John Sutter and a Wider West

John A. Sutter. Undated daguerrotype, ca. 1857, photographer unknown. Courtesy of the California Section, California State Library.

Edited by Kenneth N. Owens

John Sutter
and a Wider West

University of Nebraska Press

Lincoln and London

Library of Congress
Cataloging-in-Publication Data
John Sutter and a wider West /
edited by Kenneth N. Owens.
p.   cm.
Based on a series of
public lectures, the Sutter lectures,
presented by California State University, Sacramento,
in cooperation with the Sacramento
History and Science Division.
Includes bibliographical references and index.
ISBN 0–8032–3560–7 (alk. paper)
1. Sutter, John Augustus, 1803–1880.
2. Pioneers—California—Biography.
3. California—Biography.
I. Owens, Kenneth N.
F865.S93J645   1994
979.4'04'092–dc20
[B]
93–36522
CIP

Contents

Preface

Many historians have taken an interest in the life of John A. Sutter, but none have been more thoughtful and impartial in attitude than the five scholars whose essays appear here. During the fall of 1990 these distinguished historians participated in a unique series of public lectures, the Sutter Lectures, presented by California State University, Sacramento, in cooperation with the Sacramento History and Science Division and other historical and business groups in the Sacramento community. This volume contains the texts of the Sutter Lectures, with minor editorial amendments and documentation added for publication purposes.

An added feature is John Sutter's own 1856 narrative of his life in California, which first put into writing Sutter's claims regarding the historical importance of his activities at New Helvetia prior to the gold rush. Set down originally for his legal agent, this statement did not become public until 1878, two years before Sutter's death, when it appeared in serial form in a San Francisco newspaper. The Grabhorn Press published the account in a fine-print limited edition in 1932. Its republication here allows John Sutter to serve as his own advocate in the court of history, a role that he often assumed during the last two decades of his life.

Planning for this lecture series began simply with the concept of celebrating the one-hundred-fiftieth anniversary of John Sutter's arrival in the Sacramento region, an anniversary to be marked by various campus and civic observances. Because of complications in scheduling the five participants, the Sutter Lectures in fact came a year later than the gala ceremonies commemorating the date—officially recognized as August 12, 1839—when John Sutter first set foot on the south bank of the American River, pitched his tents, drew up three small cannons, and opened New Helvetia for business. Even so, preserving the gala spirit, we may say that the Sutter Lectures perhaps marked the sesquicentennial of the first adobe construction at Sutter's Fort, or even the one-hundred-fiftieth anniversary of John Sutter's managing somehow to pay off his first California debt—for cattle that he had secured on credit from Don Ygnacio Martínez. (Other notable events of 1840 included two campaigns by Sutter and his well-armed supporters against local native peoples, a point not entirely ignored amidst the community festivities.)

A remarkable example of town and gown cooperation, the Sutter Lectures brought intellectual substance to Sacramento's recognition of the region's most prominent historical figure. Guided by no prescribed interpretation, each speaker approached Sutter's career from a different perspective, and each contributed to a substantial reappraisal of this man and his place in western American history. If the lectures shared a central theme, it was simply the idea summed up by the title of this volume: John A. Sutter deserves renewed attention as an agent of Euro-American expansion, since he led the way for commercial enterprise and settlement in California's Central Valley, with Sutter's Fort at its strategic center. In more ways than he knew, Sutter helped link this interior country to a rapidly developing world economy, making it a significant part of a wider American West.

From the outset, the speakers shared with the lecture organizer an intention to present these talks in published form. During the course of arranging and staging the lectures, then seeing them into print, many individuals and groups contributed to the success of this project. A generous acknowledgment must go first to Robert Jones, Vice-President of University Relations at California State University, Sacramento, who originally put forward the suggestion for a lecture series, and who expedited the major financial underwriting provided by the university. Substantial funding also came from the Sacramento City-County History and Science Division and the Sacramento History Museum, through the good offices of James Henley and Kathryn Gaeddert. The Great Western Bank added important financial support through its program of community-directed contributions. In addition, the Sutter's Fort docents assisted in funding the lectures, their sponsorship demonstrating the vitality of history in this community. Special thanks are also due the Blue Diamond Growers for making available the Almond Plaza auditorium, an ideal setting for two of the Sutter Lectures.

President Donald R. Gerth of California State University, Sacramento, who has effectively promoted the university's cultural leadership in California's capital metropolis, publicly introduced the lecture series. Karyn Domich lent to the project her good spirits and charm as well as her executive skills in handling financial details and related matters. Among other key participants, graduate students in the Capital Campus Public History Program tactfully allowed themselves to be volunteered for a variety of duties that assured the effectiveness of the operation. George Petershagen, Eileen Kerr, Jerry Rouillard, Jay Correia, Susan Douglass, and Julia Hathaway all made the Sutter Lectures an important noncredit addition to their graduate curriculum, and in the course of events they became skilled practitioners of the postlecture dessert ritual.

In preparing the lectures for publication, the editor has relied on the assistance of willing friends. Two experts with a blue pencil, Melinda Peak and Sally Owens, added their skilled judgment to the editorial process. Sherry Hatch of the Sacramento History and Science Division aided the selection of illustrations for this volume, and Kathryn Stanton designed the map of John Sutter's California. The cordial cooperation of the lecturers made the editorial task a pleasant one, while the enthusiasm for the project shown by Dan Ross and his associates at the University of Nebraska Press has helped assure a relatively trouble-free publication process.

In contrast with John Sutter when he arrived in 1839, the five lecturers needed no cannons to assure their welcome or sustain their authority at New Helvetia in 1990. Large and appreciative audiences attended their talks, applauded their presentations, and afterward pressed them with questions and comments. These scholars have made important statements about Sutter. In the process, they have added to our understanding of a local heritage that links this one small area of the American West with a broadly conceived sense of history. It is a pleasure now to make their research and conclusions generally available; because of their work, we can all better appreciate the true dimensions of John Sutter's accomplishments within the context of both his own time and ours, even as we recognize more clearly the personal imperfections that figured so largely in his career.

General Sutter's Diary

Editor's Note: Written by John Sutter for his legal adviser in May or June of 1856, this autobiographical account appeared in a San Francisco weekly newspaper entitled *The Argonaut* early in 1878, serialized in four consecutive editions beginning on January 26. According to *The Argonaut*'s editor, the manuscript had come to light in the papers of one of the state's eminent men, recently deceased—presumably Sutter's lawyer at one time—and his widow had made it available for publication. Subsequently the original manuscript disappeared, so we have only the newspaper version as a source; but according to his own statement, the editor of *The Argonaut* attempted "to preserve, as nearly as was practicable, the quaint phraseology, erroneous orthography, and imperfect punctuation of the manuscript. . . ." For one familiar with Sutter's letters and other writings, the account's language, tone, and detail of incident all sustain the authenticity of the document in this form.

In *The Argonaut* this account appeared under the heading "General Sutter's Diary: Some Hitherto Unpublished Chapters of Early California History." Obviously the title is a misnomer, since the text consists of Sutter's reminiscences of his years in California, written in the form of a narrative statement—though comparison indicates that apparently his memory was aided in part by reference to the document known as the New Helvetia Diary, a manuscript now found among the holdings of the Society of California Pioneers Library.

Using the text in *The Argonaut* as a basis, the Grabhorn Press of San

Francisco brought out a limited edition of this narrative in 1932, entitling it *The Diary of Johann August Sutter*. Supplemented with a biographical preface by Douglas S. Watson, this publication included reproductions of portraits of both John Sutter and Anna Dübeld Sutter then owned by their granddaughter, Mrs. M. Van Wolbeck of San Francisco. It also contained reproductions of an 1847 lithographic view of Sutter's Fort and a reproduction of a Sutter's Fort military roster for January 1, 1845, both from originals in the collection of Edwin Grabhorn. The press issued five hundred copies of this publication, assuring that it would remain relatively rare.

The present edition, also based on the text as it appeared in *The Argonaut*, differs in small ways from the Grabhorn Press version. Both versions correct obvious typographical errors in the original, and both contain parenthetical insertions made by John Sutter. The bracketed insertions represent new editorial amendments, added to this version for clarity's sake. Since Sutter tended to carry into English certain nineteenth-century German forms of punctuation, particularly by using a comma at places that require a period according to customary usage, this edition in a few instances also silently alters the punctuation of the original for the purpose of clarity, and it supplies paragraphing where appropriate for added intelligibility and consistency. In all other respects, the document represents exactly the Sutter statement published by *The Argonaut* in 1878, maintaining the diacritical marks of the original and ignoring a few textual changes made by Douglas Watson for the 1932 edition. To avoid future confusion, this edition also adheres to the original title, however inappropriate.

This account has particular importance in documenting John Sutter's career, for it represents his first substantial effort to set down in writing the story of his California career. Composed less than a decade after many of the events he describes, the narrative demonstrates that Sutter had already begun to portray himself as the heroic founder of civilization in the Sacramento region, meanwhile overstating the importance of his services in helping the United States government take California from Mexico and claiming exaggerated credit for the gold discovery. On his own authority, he affirmed that he had been a person of great foresight and energy whose wondrous accomplishments had finally brought him to the brink of immense success. But then, Sutter claimed, he had been betrayed by fortune, and swindled and robbed by many unscrupulous people who were able to profit from his enterprise.

Even before the era of gold-rush prosperity had ended, this account tells us, John Sutter had invented for himself a new role. Utterly lacking a sense of irony or any recognition of his own failings, Sutter here built on his lifelong skill in finding excuses for financial delinquencies to claim the honor of being California's foremost living historical relic, a hapless victim of his own incompetent fiscal management and the greed of others, who yet deserved wide appreciation and generous public recompense for his pioneer services. With this account, not originally meant for a public audience, the Sutter myth made its appearance fresh from the hand of its creator.

As his disappointments continued to accumulate, confirming his shortcomings both as a businessman and in personal relationships, John Sutter rehearsed his mythical role again and again. He played it to perfection in his petitions to Congress and in the more detailed autobiographical account that he dictated to Hubert Howe Bancroft in 1876. Struggling to survive in later years, Sutter continued to assert his undiminished belief in the myth. It bolstered his claim to public reward, as Bancroft was the first to observe, for activities that he had earlier pursued—though at times ineptly and erratically—in expectation of private profit. Yet, as suggested by some of the scholars whose essays follow in this volume, the Sutter myth served other purposes as well, purposes that long outlived John Sutter. It well may have become his most enduring legacy.

The Statement of Johann August Sutter, 1856

Left the State of Missouri (where I had resided for a many years) on the 1th a April, 1838, and travelled with the party of Men under Capt. Tripps [Andrew Drips], of the Amer. fur Compy, to their Rendezvous in the Rocky Mountains (Wind River Valley); from there I travelled with 6 brave Men to Oregon, as I considered myself not strong enough to cross the Sierra Nevada and go direct to California (which was my intention from my first Start on having got some informations from a Gent'n in New Mexico, who has been in California).

Under a good Many Dangers and other troubles I have passed the Different forts or trading posts of the Hudsons Bay Compy. and arrived at the Mission at the Dalls on Columbia River. From this place I crossed right strait through thick & thin and arrived to the great astonishment of the inhabitants. I arrived in 7 days in the Valley of the Willamette, while others with good guides arrived only in 17 days previous [to] my Crossing.

At fort Vancouver I has been very hospitably received and invited to pass the Winter with the Gentlemen of the [Hudson's Bay] Company, but as a Vessel of the Compy. was ready to sail for the Sandwich Islands [Hawaii], I took a passage in her, in hopes to get Soon a Passage from there to California, but 5 long Months I had to wait to find an Opportunity to leave, but not direct to California, except far out of my Way to the Russian American Colonies on the North West Coast, to Sitka the Residence of the Gov'r, (Lat. 57).

I remained one Month there and delivered the Cargo of the Brig Clementine, as I had Charge of the Vessel, and then sailed down the Coast in heavy Gales, and entered in Distress in the Port of San Francisco, on the 2d of July 1839. An Officer and 15 Soldiers came on board and ordered me out, saying that Monterey is the Port of entry, & at last [that] I could obtain 48 hours to get provisions (as we were starving) and some repairings done on the Brig.

In Monterey I arranged my affairs with the Custum House, and presented myself to Govr. Alvarado, and told him my intention to Settle here in this Country, and that I have brought with me 5 White Men and 8 Kanacas [Hawaiians] (two of them married). 3 of the Whitemen were Mechanics, he was very glad to hear that, and particularly when I told him, that I intend to Settle in the interior on the banks of the river Sacramento, because the Indians then at this time would not allow white Men and particularly of the Spanish Origin to come near them, and was very hostile, and stole the horses from the inhabitants, near San José. I got a General passport for my small Colony and permission to select a Territory where ever I would find it convenient, and to come in one Years time again in Monterey to get my Citizenship and the title of the Land, which I have done so, and not only this, I received a high civil Office ("Representante del Govierno en las fronteras del Norte, y Encargado de la Justicia").

When I left Yerba buena (now San Francisco) after having leaved the Brig and dispatched her back to the S[andwich] I[slands], I bought several small Boats (Launches) and Chartered the Schooner "Isabella" for my Exploring Journey to the inland Rivers and particularly to find the Mouth of the River Sacramento, as I could find Nobody who could give me information, only that they Knew that some very large Rivers are in the interior.

It took me eight days before I could find the entrance of the Sacramento, as it is very deceiving and very easy to pass by, how it happened to several Officers of the Navy afterwards which refused to take a pilot. About 10 miles below Sacramento City I fell in with the first Indians which was all armed & painted & looked very hostile. They was about 200 Men, as some of them understood a little Spanish I could make a Kind of treaty with them, and the two which understood Spanish came with me, and made me a little better acquainted with the Country. All other Indians on the up River hided themselves in the Bushes, and on the Mouth of Feather River they runned all away so soon they discovered us.

I was examining the Country a little further up with a Boat, while the large Crafts let go their Ankers. On my return all the white Men came to me and asked me how much longer I intended to travell with them in such a Wilderness. I saw plain that it was a Mutiny. I answered them that I would give them an answer the next Morning and left them and went in the Cabin.

The following Morning I gave Orders to return, and entered in the American River, landed at the former Tannery on the 12th Augt. 1839. Gave Orders to get every thing on Shore, pitch the tents and mount the 3 Cannons, called the white Men, and told them that all those which are not contented could leave on board the Isabella, next Morning and that I would settle with them imediately, and remain alone with the Canacas, of 6 Men 3 remained, and 3 of them I gave passage to Yerba buena.

The Indians was first troublesome, and came frequently, and would it not have been for the Cannons they would have Killed us for the sake of my property, which they liked very much, and this intention they had very often, how they have confessed to me afterwards, when on good terms. I had a large Bull Dog which saved my life 3 times, when they came slyly near the house in the Night: he got hold of and marked them most severely. In a short time removed my Camps on the very spot where now the Ruins of Sutters fort stands, made acquaintance with a few Indians which came to work for a short time making

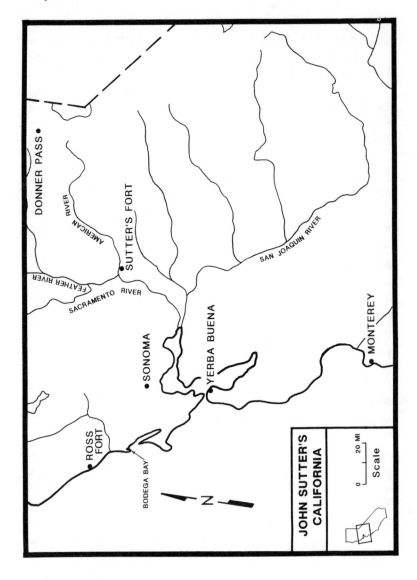

JOHN SUTTER'S CALIFORNIA

Adobés, and the Canacas was building 3 grass houses, like it is customary on the Sandwich Islands. Before I came up here, I purchased Cattle & Horses on the Rancho of Señor Martinez, and had great difficulties & trouble to get them up, and had to wait for them [a] long time, and received them at least on the 22d October 1839. Not less than 8 Men wanted to be in the party, as they were afraid of the Indians, and had good reasons to be so.

Before I got the Cattle we was hunting Deer & Elk etc. and so [continued] afterwards to safe the Cattle as I had then only about 500 head, 50 horses & a manada of 25 mares. One Year [later], that is in the fall 1840, I bought 1000 head of Cattle of Don Antonio Suñol and a many horses more of Don Joaquin Gomez and others. In the fall 1839 I have built an Adobe house, covered with Tule and two other small buildings which [were] in the middle of the fort; they was afterwards destroyed by fire. At the same time we cut a Road through the Woods [to] where the City of Sacramento stand[s], then we made the New Embarcadero, where the old Zinkhouse stands now. After this it was time to make a Garden, and to sow some Wheat &c. We broke up the soil with poor Californian ploughs, I had a few Californians employed as Baqueros [vaqueros], and 2 of them making Cal. Carts & stocking the ploughs etc.

In the Spring 1840 the Indians began to be troublesome all around me, Killing and Wounding Cattle, stealing horses, and threatening to attack us en Mass. I was obliged to make Campaigns against them and punish them severely, a little later about 2 a [to] 300 was aproching and got United on Cosumne River, but I was not waiting for them. Left a small Garrison at home, Canons & other Arms loaded, and left with 6 brave men & 2 Baquero's in the night, and took them by surprise at Day light. The fighting was a little hard, but after having lost about 30 men, they was willing to make a treaty with me, and after this leçon they behaved very well, and became my best friends and Soldiers, with which I has been assisted to conquer the whole Sacramento and a part of the San Joaquin Valley.

They became likewise tolerable good laborers and the boys had to learn mechanical trades; teamster's, Vaquero's, etc. At the time the Communication with the Bay was very long and dangerous, particularly in open Boats; it is a great Wonder that we got not swamped a many times, all [the] time with an Indian Crew and a Canaca at the helm. Once it took me (in December 1839) 16 days to go down to Yerba buena and to return. I went down again on the 22d Xber [December] [18]39 to Yerba buena and on account of the inclemency of the Weather and the strong current in the River I need a whole month (17 days coming up) and nearly all the provisions spoiled.

March the 18th [1840] dispatched a party of White men and Indians in serch for pine timber and went not further up on the Amer. River as about 25 miles, found and cut some but not of a good quality and rafted it down the River. On the end of the month of March there was an other conspiracy of some Indians, but was soon quelled when I succeeded to disarm them.

August 17th 1840. The men who crossed with me the Rocky Mountains [Niklaus Allgeier and Sebastian Keyser] with two others had a chance to come from Oregon on board an Amer. Vessel which landed them at Bodega, at the time occupied by the Russians. When they told the Russian Governor that they wanted to join me, he received them very kindly and hospitable, furnished them with fine horses, new Saddles etc. at a very low rate and gave them direction whereabout they would have to travell, without being seen by some Spaniards, which would have them brought to Sonoma in the prison, and after a many difficulties they found me at last. I was of Course very glad having these brave men again with me, and employed them, and so I became strong at once.

On the 23d Augt., 1841 Capt. Ringold of Comadore Wilkse Exploring Squadron, arrived on the Embarcadero, piloted by one of the Launches Indian crew; without this they would not have found so easy the entrance of the Sacramento. They had 6 Whaleboats & 1 Launch, 7 Officers and about 50 men in all. I was very glad indeed to see them, sent immediately saddled horses for the Officers, and my Clerk with an invitation to come and see me. At their arrival I fired a salut, and furnished them what they needed. They was right surprised to find me up here in this Wilderness. It made a very good impression upon the Indians to see so many whites are coming to see me. They surveyed the River as far as the [Sutter] Butes.

September 4th 1841. Arrived the Russian Govr. Mr. Alexander Rottiheff [Rotchev] on board the Schooner Sacramento, and offered me their whole Establishment at Bodega & Ross for sale, and invited me to come right of[f] with him, as there is a Russian Vessel at Bodega, and some Officers with plein [plenary] power, to transact this business with me, and particularly they would give me the preference, as they became all acquainted with me, during a months stay at Sitka. I left and went with him down to the Bay in Company with Capt. Ringold's Expedition. What for a fleet we thought then, is on the River. Arriving at Bodega, we came very soon to terms, from there we went to fort Ross where they showed me everything and returned to Bodega again, and before the Vessel sailed we dined on board the Helena, and closed the bargain for $30,000, which has been paid. And other property, was a separate account which has been first paid.

On the 28th of September I dispatched a number of men and my Clerk by Land to Bodega, to receive the Cattle, Horses, Mules & Sheep, to bring them up to Sutter's fort, called then New Helvetia. By crossing the Sacramento the[y] lost me from about 2000 head about a 100, which drowned in the River, but of most of them we could safe the hides, our Cal. Banknotes at the time.

I did send a Clark with some men in charge of these Establishments [at Bodega Bay and Fort Ross] and left the necessary horses and Cattle there. The Schooner Sacramento keept up the communication between the Coast and here, and brought me as freight the Lumber, to finish the House in the fort. I was just building and errecting the fort at the time in Aug. & Sept. [1841] for protection of [against] the Indians and of [against] the Californians which became very jealous seeing these fortifications and 12 Canons and a field piece mounted, and two other brass pieces unmounted at the time.

October 18th, 1841. A party of Comodore Wilks' Exploring Squadron, arrived from Oregon by land, consisting of the Scientific Corps, a few Naval Officers, Marine Soldiers and Mountaineers as Guides under Command of Lieut. Emmons. I received them so well as I could, and then the Scientific Corps left by Land for San José and the Naval Officers & Marines I dispatched them on board of one of my Vessels.

[The period from October 1841 to March 1844 is blank in this account. This same period receives only brief, general coverage in the more detailed Sutter narrative dictated to Hubert Howe Bancroft in 1876, now found in the collections of the Bancroft Library, University of California, Berkeley.]

March 6th 1842 [1844]. Captain [John Charles] Frémont arrived at the fort with Kit Carson, told me that he was an officer of the U. S. and left a party behind in Distress and on foot, the few surviving Mules was packed only with the most necessary. I received him politely and his Company likewise as an old acquaintance. The next Morning I furnished them with fresh horses, & a Vaquero with a pack Mule loaded with Necessary Supplies for his Men. Capt. Frémont found in my Establishment every thing what he needed, that he could travell without Delay. He could have not found it so by [going to] a Spaniard, [only] perhaps by [going to] a great Many and with loosing a great deal of time. I sold him about 60 Mules & about 25 horses, and fat young Steers or Beef Cattle, all the Mules & horses got Shoed. On the 23d March, all was ready and on the 24th he left with his party for the U. States.

As an Officer of the Govt. it was my duty to report to the Govt., that Capt. Frémont arrived. Genl. Micheltorena dispatched Lieut. Col. Telles (afterwards Gov. of Sinaloa) with [a] Capt., Lieut., and 25 Dragoons, to inquire what Captain Frémonts business was here; but he was en route as they arrive[d] only on the 27th.

From this time on Exploring, Hunting & Trapping parties has been started. At the same time Agricultural & Mechanical business was progressing from Year to year, and more Notice has been taken of my establishment. It became even a fame, and some early Distinguished Travellers like Doctor Sandells, Wasnesensky & others, Captains of Trading Vessels & Super Cargos, even Californians (after the Indians was subdued) came and paid me a visit, and was astonished to see what for Work of all kinds has been done. Small Emigrant parties arrived, and brought me some very valuable Men. With one of those was Major Bidwell (he was about 4 Years in my employ). Major Reading & Major Hensley with 11 other brave Men arrived alone, both of those Gentlemen has been 2 Years in my employ. With these parties excellent Mechanics arrived which was all employed by me, likewise good farmers. We made imediately Amer. ploughs in my Shops and [had] all kind of work done. Every year the Russians was bound to furnish me with good iron & Steel & files, Articles which could not be got here, likewise Indian Beeds and the most important of all was 100 lb. of fine Rifle & 100 lb. of Canon powder, and several 100 lb. of Lead (every year). With these I was carefull like with Gold.

From the Hudson Bay Company I received likewise great supplies, and particularly Powder, lead, and Shot, Beaver Trapps and Clothing (on Credit, to be paid for in Beaver and Otter Skins). They would not have done this to [for] everyone; but as I has been highly recommended to these gentlemen from England and personally acquainted, they have done so. Once I received a visit of Mr. Douglas, who was the Commander in Chief of the [Hudson's Bay Company] establishments on the Pacific & the mountains, after Dr. McLaughlin resigned.

With such a supply of Powder, Ammunition & Arms, I made a bold appearance. The fort was built in about 4 years of time, as it was very difficult to get the necessary lumber. We was sawing by hand Oak timber. Under Gen'l Micheltorena our Govr. I received the rank and Title Capt. of the Mexican Army. He found it his Policy to be [a] friend with me, as he was all [the] time threatened with a Revolution of the Californians notwithstanding having about 1000 troupes (Mexicans). Having the rank as Capt. and Military Comander of the Northern frontieres, I began to drill the Indians, with the assistance of two good Non Commissioned Officers from my Country, which I promoted to Capt. & first Lieut't & got their Comissions and from the time I had a self-made Garrison, but the Soldiers to earn for their Uniforms & food etc. had to work when they was not on Duty.

During this time my Stock was increasing; had about then 8000 head of Cattle and 2000 horses and breeding Mares and about 4000 Sheep. Of the Wool we made our own Plankets, as we established under great Difficulties a factory. Plankets, like nearly all other articles was very scarce and sold to very high prices at the time.

Emigration continued in small parties, just strong enough to protect themselves travelling through a Country of hostile Indians, all of them was allways hospitably received under my roof and all those who could or would not be employed, could stay with me so long as they liked, and when leaving, I gave them Passports which was everywhere respected. [When there] Was some trouble below all came immediately to me for protection. Of the different unfortunate Emigrations which suffered so much in the Snow, it is unnecessary to speak of, as it was published in the papers throughout the States.

In the fall 1844, I went to Monterey with Major Bidwell and a few armed men (Cavallada & Servants) how it was customary to travell at these times, to pay a Visit to Gen'l Micheltorena. I has been received with greatest Civil and Military honors. One day he gave a great

Diner, after Diner all the Troupes were parading, and in the evening a balloon was sent to the higher regions, etc., etc.

At the time it looked very gloomy. The people of the Country was arming and preparing to make a Revolution, and I got some sure and certain information, of the British Consul and other Gentlemen of my acquaintance, which I visited on my way to Monterey. They did not know that the General and myself were friends, and told and discovered [to] me the whole plan, that in a short time the people of the Country will be ready to blockade the General and his troupes in Monterey, and then take him prisoner and send him and his Soldiers back to Mexico, and make a Gov'r of [someone from among] their own people etc. I was well aware what we could expect should they succeed to do this; they would drive us foreigners all very soon out of the Country, how they have done it once, in the winter [of] 1839. Capt. Vioget has already been engaged by Castro & Alvarado to be ready with his vessel to take the Gen'l and his Soldiers to Mexico.

I had a confidential Conversation with Genl. Micheltorena who received me with great honors and Distinction in Monterey. After [my] having him informed of all what is going on in the Country, he took his measures in a Counsel of war in which I has been present. I received my Orders to raise such a large auxiliary force as I possibly could, and to be ready at his Order, at the same time I received some Cartridges and some small Arms which I had ship[p]ed on board the Alert, and took a Passage myself for San francisco (or then Yerba buena). If I had travelled by land, Castro would have taken me a Prisoner in San Juan, where he was laying in Ambush for me. In Yerba buena I remained only a few hours as my Schooner was ready to receive me on board, having waited for me at Y[erb]a B[uen]a. I visited the Officers of the Custom house and Castro's Officer, which immediately after I left received an Order to arrest me, but I was under fair Way to Sacramento.

After my Arrival at the fort, I began to organize a force for the General, regular Drill of the Indian Infanterie took place, the Mounted Rifle Company about 100 Men of all Nations was raised, of which Capt. Gantt was the Commander; as all was under fair way and well organized, and joint with a Detachment of California Cavallry (which deserted from Vallejo) we left the fort with Music and flying Colors on the 1th January 1845, to join the General, and comply with his Orders.

Major Reading was left with a small Garrison of Frenchmen, Canadians and Indians, as Commander of the upper Country.

Castro had his Headquarters then in the Mission of San José. He did not expect us so soon, as he was just commencing to fortify himself. He ran away with his Garrison, was collecting a stronger force, and want[ed] to trouble us on our March, but as he saw I was on a good Qui Vive for him, he left for Monterey to unite with the forces that was blockading the General and his troops in Monterey, and advanced or runed for the lower Country, to call or force the people there to take Arms against the Government.

On the Salinas River near Monterey the Genl. was encamped with our united force, about 600 Men (he left a Garrison in Monterey) we pursued the enemy, and had to pursue him down to Los Angeles. The first encounter we had with the enemy was at Buenaventura, where we attacked him and drove them out [of] their comfortable quarters.

While at and near Santa Barbara, a great Many of Soldiers of my Division Deserted, over 50 men of the Mounted Rifles, the Detachment of Cala. Cavalry deserted and joined their Countrymen the Rebells, likewise a good number of the Mexican Dragoons.

Near San Fernando (Mission) the enemy occupied a fine position, and appeared in full strength, joined by a company of American Traders coming from Sonora and another Company of the same consisting of Traders and Trappers and the whole force of the enemy was over [one] thousand Men, well provided with everything, and our force has been no more as about 350 or 375 Men, and during the battle of Cahuenga near San fernando, the balance of the Mounted Riflemen, and the Artillerie deserted, and myself fell in the hands of the enemy and was taken prisoner and transported to Los Angeles.

A few days after this, the General, surrounded by the enemy, so that he could get nothing more to eat, capitulated, and after the necessary Documents was signed by both parties, the Genl. was allowed to march with Music and flying colours to San Pedro, where some vessels was ready to take him and his troops on board, and after having delivered their arms etc. proceeded up to Monterey to take [to Mexico] the remaining Garrison, the family of the General and his privat property, likewise the families of some of the officers. This was the End of the reign of Genl. Govr. Manl. Micheltorena.

The new Govt. under Gov. Pio Pico, and General Castro, etc. had the intention to shoot me. They was of the Oppinion, that I had joined Genl. Micheltorena Voluntarely, but so soon as I could get my Baggage and my papers, I could prove and show by the Orders of my General that I have obeied his Orders, and done my Duty to the legal Government. And so I was acquitted with all honors, and confirmed in my former Offices as Military Commander of the Northern frontier, and exchanged [encharged] with the [administration of] Justice, with the expressed wish that I might be so faithful to the new Govt. as I had been to Genl. Micheltorena.

While [I] was in Santa Barbara I had a Conversation with Genl. Micheltorena, in reference of the expense, etc., because at the time I had already an Account of about $8000, without counting a cent for my own services, and for my whole rendered services from [the] beginning of my different Offices which I held under Alvarado & the Genl. never they have paid me, even for a Courier, and never furnished me with a Govts. horse. The General told me that he knew this very well, and as he had no money, he would let me have some land, and even if I should like the sobrante [grant] for which I [had] applied when last in Monterey, and which Document was mislaid or destroyed by Dn. Manuel Timeno. I told him that I would be contented, and as we are in Campaign and might be killed by the enemy I wish that the Document would be writen in the name of my eldest Son and my whole family.

The Genl. did send for one of his Aid[es]-de-Camp Capt. Casteñeda, who was acting Secretary. This Gentleman wrote the Document (he is alife yet), he has given his testimony before the Land Commission about 2 years ago. This Document with a many others has been given to John S. Fowler in Care while he was acting as my Agent, and [it] was afterwards destroyed by fire.

After a return of hardship from San Fernando through Tularé Valley, we turned all out again to our former Occupations, and arrived at the fort on the 11th April 1845.

27th Septr. [1845] A large party of emigrants arrived. On the 30th dispatched a party of men to assist them.

October 7th. An other large party arrived (about 60 Wagons). Visitors and letters from the U. States.

October 21th. Received Bandas (Proclamations) and Orders of Governor Pio Pico and Genl. Castro. This was on account rumors was circulating that war had been declared between the U. States and Mexico. On the 23d a Meeting was held of the Emigrants at the Fort (Thursday). After the Proclamations had been translated to the Meeting, they adjourned over until Monday next.

Novr 11th 1845 was the Day when the Commissioner from Mexico, Don Andrés Castillero arrived at the Fort in Company with Genl. Dn. José Castro, Col. Prudon, Ma[jor] Lees[e], staff and Escort of Castro. A salut was fired.

After having refused to let them have the fort for $100,000 or for Castros offer for the Mission of San José etc., etc., they left the next day. Salut fired.

December 10th. [1845] Capt. J. C. Frémont arrived again.

December 12th. Delivered him 14 mules.

December 13th. [Frémont's command] left for the South to meet Capt. J. Walker. On the same day, two Blacksmiths of Frémonts arrived, to take charge of one of the Blacksmith Shops, to make Horse Shoes Nails etc.

December 23th. Indians was driving of[f] Stock, some of it we got back again.

December 25th 1845. Arrived Capt. W. L. [Lansford W.] Hastings direct from the U. States crossing the Mountains with 11 men. Among them was Doctor Semple. If they had arrived one day later they would have been cut of[f] by the immense quantity of Snow. I keept the whole party over winter, some of them I employed.

January 14th 1846, Capt. Leidesdorff U. S. vice Consul & Capt. Hinckley, Capt. of the Port of San francisco, arrived on a friendly Visit. On the 15th January Capt Frémont returned, not beeing able to find Capt. Walker. As we were two officers of the Mex. Govt. with the Vice Consul of the U.S. we put ourselves in Uniform, and visited Frémont in his Camp, and invited him to dine with us at the Fort, which he accepted, put himself in Uniform and joint us, as we approached the Fort a salut was fired.

January 17th 1846, Supplied Frémonts Camp with Provisions.

January 19th. Capt. Frémont with 8 of his men took passage on board my Schooner for Yerba buena.

January 30th. Received a Visit of Major Snyder and Mr. Sublette, they brought the News of War being declared between the U.S. & England.

February 19th. News was sent to me that no Mexican Troopes has arrived, which were daily expected in the Country, and that probably California is about to be delivered up to the U. S.

March 14th. Doctor Marsh sent an Express with information of Frémonts Difficulties with Castro. Capt. Frémont was blockaded near Monterey by Castro and his Troopes, and [Castro] refused [to let] him to proceed to the South through the Country on the Coste, etc. The foreign Residents wanted to assist Frémont, but he refused their aid.

March 21th. Capt. Frémont returned and camped on the other side of the Amer. Fork, and looking out for the Californians, and in a few days left for the upper Sacramento, and for Oregon.

April 28th. Arrived Lieut. A. Gillespie of the U. States Marine Corps, who had secret Dispatches for Frémont, and wanted to overtake him on his route to Oregon. I furnished him with Animals. He went up to Peter Lassens with my Guide. At P. Lassens he hired Men and bought Animals to overtake Frémont. After a sharp riding he succeeded to overtake him, and returned with him to the Sacramento Valley.

May 25th. Saml. Neal passed on a secret errant for Monterey.

May 30th, 1846. Lieut. A. Gillespie arrived from the Upper Sacramento Valley, and left on the 1st June on board my Schooner for Yerba buena.

June 3d. I left in Company of Major Reading, and most all of the Men in my employ, for a Campaign with the Mukelemney Indians, which has been engaged by Castro and his Officers to revolutionize all the Indians against me, to Kill all the foreigners, burn their houses and Wheat fields etc. These Mukelemney Indians had great promesses and some of them were finely dressed and equiped, and those came apparently on a friendly visit to the fort and Vicinity and had long Conversation with the influential Men of the Indians, and one Night a Number of them entered in my Potrero (a kind of enclosed pasture) and was Ketching horses to drive the whole Cavallada away with them. The Sentinel at the fort heard the distant Noise of these Horses, and gave due notice, & imediately I left with about 6 well armed Men and attacked them, but they could make their escape in the Woods (where Sac. City stands now) and so I left a guard with the horses. As we had to cross the Mukelemney River on rafts, one of those rafts capsized with 10 Rifles, and 6 prs. of Pistols, a good supply of Amunition, and the Clothing of about 24 Men, and Major Reading & another Man nearly drowned.

Some Men remained on the dry places as they had no Clothing nor Arms, the remaining Arms and amunitions has been divided among the whole, and so we marched the whole Night on the Calaveras [River], and could not find the enemy. In the Morning by Sunrise we took a little rest, and soon dispatched a party to discover and recon-noitre the enemy. A Dog came to our Camp which was a well known dog of the Mukelemneys, a sign that they are not very far from us. At the same time a Courier of the party came on galloping, telling us that the party fell already in an engagem[en]t with the enemy. Imediately we left galloping to join in the fight; already some of our Men was wounded and unable to fight. We continued the fighting until they re-tired and fled in a large hole like a Cellar in the bank of the Calaveras, covered with brushes and trees, firing and shooting with their bows and arrows, but we had them blockaded, and killed them a good many of their Men, but on account of having no more powder and balls, we found it very prudent to leave the Scene slowly, so that it appeared as we wanted to Camp, and so we made a forced March and Crossed the Mukelemney, and returned from this Campaign on the 7th June.

June 8th. Arrived Lieut. Francisco Arcé with 8 Soldiers & Govt. horses from Sonoma for Genl. Castro.

June 9th. Departed Lieutenant Arcé for Monterey.

June 10th. A party of Americans under Command of E. Merritt, took all the horses from Arcé at Murphey's.

June 13th. The Portsmouths Launch arrived under Command of Lieut. Hunter, in Company with Lieut. Gillespie, Purser Waldron & Doctor Duvall.

June 14th. Lieut. Gillespie & Hensley left for Frémont's Camp near Hock farm.

June 16th. [Ezekiel] Merritt & Kitt Carson arrived with News of Sonoma beeing occupied by the Americans, and the same evening ar-rived as prissoners Genl. Vallejo, Don Salvador Vallejo, Lt. Col. Pru-don & M[ajor] Leese, and given under my charge and Care. I have treated them with kindness and so good as I could, which was re-ported to Frémont, and he then told me that prissoners ought not to be treated so, then I told him, if it is not right how I treat them, to give them in charge of somebody else.

June 17th. Departed the Portsmouth Launch for Yerba buena. Capt. Frémont moved Camp up to the Amer. fork, a good many people joining Frémonts Camp.

June 18th. Arrived Express from Sonoma with letter from Capt. Montgomery.

June 19th. Arrived Capt. Frémont with about 20 Men from Camp. José Noriega was detained prissoner. Frémonts Blacksmiths were busily engaged. Vicente Peralta, who was up in the Valley on a visit, was detained prissoner.

June 21st. Capt Frémont & Camp deposited the Packs and then camped across Amer. fork. Major Reading and my Trappers joined the Camp, and left for Sonoma as a strong Detachment of Californians crossed the Estrecho de Carqinas [Carquinez Strait] at Benicia.

June 26th. Lieut. Revere & Dr. Henderson of the [U.S. Navy ship] Portsmouth with a party of Men arrived in a Man of War Boat. A party of Men arrived from Oregon by land, which joined Frémont.

June 28th. Arrived Lieut. Bartlett of the Portsmouth and organized a Garrison.

July 10th. [Frémont] arrived or returned from Sonoma with his Company. On this trip or Campaign to Sonoma some cruel actions has been done on both sides.

Capt. Montgomery did send an Amer. flag by Lieut. Revere then in Command of Sonoma, and some dispatches to Frémont, I received the Order to hiss [hoist] the flag by Sunrise from Lt. Revere. Long time before daybreak, I got ready with loading the Canons and when it was day the roaring of the Canons got the people all stirring. Some of them made long faces, as they thought if the Bear flag would remain there would be a better chance to rob and plunder. Capt. Frémont received Orders to proceed to Monterey with his forces. Capt. Montgomery provided for the upper Country, established Garrisons in all important places, Yerba buena, Sonoma, San José, and fort Sacramento. Lieut. Missroon came to organize our Garrison better and [enlist] more Numbers of white Men and Indians of my former Soldiers, and gave me the Command of this Fort. The Indians have not yet received their pay yet for their services, only each one [getting] a shirt and a pre. of pants, & abt. 12 men got Coats.

So went the War on in California. Capt. Frémont was nearly all [the] time engaged in the lower Country and made himself Governor, until Genl. Kearny arrived, when an other Revolution took place. And Frémont for disobeying Orders was made prissoner by Genl. Kearny, who took him afterwards with him to the U. States by Land across the Mountains.

After the War I was anxious that Business should go on like before, and on the 28th May, 1847, Marshall & Gingery, two Millwrights, I employed to survey the large Millraise for the Flour Mill at Brighton.

May 24th. Lieut't Anderson arrived with a Detachment of Stevenson's Regiment of N. Y. Volunteers for a Garrison, and to relieve my Indian Soldiers from their Service.

May 31st. Mr. Marshall commenced the great work of the large Millraise, with ploughs and scrapers.

June 13th. A visit of Genl Kearny and his Staff and a few other Gentlemen. A salut was fired and the Garrison was parading.

June 14th. A diner given to Gen'l Kearny and Staff. Capt. Frémont a prisoner of Gen'l Kearny. Walla Walla Indian Chiefs and people visited Frémont and wanted their pay for Services rendered in the Campaign when they was with Frémonts Battaillon, he then ordered one of his officers to pay them with Govt's horses. (Horses which has been taken from the people of the Country was called Govt. horses and war horses).

June 16th. Gen'l Kearny, Staff & Escort etc. left for the U. States across the Mountains.

June 22nd. The Walla Walla Indians have done a great deal of Depredations on their return march to Oregon, stole horses of mine and other people, stole from a many Indian tribes and maltreated them. They are a very bad Tribe of Indians and very warlike.

July 17th, 18th & 19th. Went on a visit to Comodore Stockton in his Camp on Bear creek. The Comodore left with a Strong party for the U. States across the Mountains. Made a present to the Comodore with my best and finest horse of my Cavallada. Great Sickness and diseases amongst the Indian tribes, and a great Number of them were dying notwithstanding of having employed a Doctor to my hospital.

July 20th. Got all the necessary timber for the frame of the mill-building.

July 21st. Left with Marshall and an Indian Chief in search for a Mill site in the Mountains.

August 2d. Major Cloud, paymaster & Capt Folsom quartermaster arrived; the former paid of[f] the Garrison at the fort. On the 4th, these two Gentlemen left on Horseback. I accompanied them, and [when] we was only but only 1/2 mile from the fort Major Cloud fell from his horse senseless and died in the evening. The Surgeon of the Garrison & my own Doctor have done what could be done to safe him. On the 6th, Major Cloud was burried with military honors. Capt. Folsom commanded the Troops, as Lieut't Anderson was sick.

August 25th. Capt Hart of the Mormon Battaillon arrived, with a good many of his Men on their Way to great Salt Lake. They had Orders for Govt. Horses, which I delivered to them, (War Horses) *not paid for yet.* They bought provisions and got Blacksmith work done. I employed about Eighty Men of them, some as Mechanics, some as laborers, on the Mill and Millraise at Brighton; some as laborers at the Sawmill at Columa.

August 28th, 1847. Marshall moved, with P. Wisners [Wimmer] family and the working hands to Columa, and began to work briskly on the sawmill.

Septr. 10th. Mr. Sam'l Brannan returned from the great Salt Lake, and announced a large Emigration by land. On the 19th the Garrison was removed, Lieut't Per Lee took her down to San francisco.

September 21st. Employed more Carpenters to assist Brouett on the Grist Mill.

October 3d. A great many Emigrants arrived, and so it continued through the whole of the month.

October 12th. A small Store was established by S'l Brannan & Smith in one of the houses near the fort.

Novr. 1th. Getting with a great deal of trouble and with breaking wagons the four Runs of Millstones, to the Mill Site (Brighton) from the Mountains.

Decembr 22. Received about 2000 fruit trees with great expenses from Fort Ross, Napa Valley and other places, which was given in Care of men who called themselves Gardeners, and nearly all of the trees was neglected by them and died.

January 28th, 1848. Marshall arrived in the evening, it was raining very heavy, but he told me he came on important business. After we was alone in a private Room he showed me the first Specimens of Gold, that is he was not certain if it was Gold or not, but he thought it might be; immediately I made the proof and found that it was Gold. I told him even that most of all is 23 Carat Gold; he wished that I should come up with him immediately, but I told him that I have to give first my orders to the people in all my factories and shops.

February 1th. Left for the Sawmill attended by a Baquero (Olimpio). Was absent 2d, 3d, 4th, & 5th. I examined myself everything and picked up a few Specimens of Gold myself in the tail race of the Sawmill; this Gold and others which Marshall and some of the other laborers gave to me (it was found while in my employ and Wages) I told them that I would a Ring got made of it so soon as a Goldsmith would be here. I had a talk with my employed people all at the Sawmill. I told them that as they do know now that this Metal is Gold, I wished that they would do me the great favor and keep it a secret only 6 weeks, because my large Flour Mill at Brighton would have been in Operation in such a time, which undertaking would have been a fortune to me, and unfortunately the people would not keep it secret, and so I lost on this Mill at the lowest calculation about $25,000.

March 7th. The first party of Mormons, employed by me left for washing and digging Gold and very soon all followed, and left me only the sick and the lame behind. And at this time I could say that every body left me from the Clerk to the Cook. What for great Damages I had to suffer in my tannery which was just doing a profitable and extensive business, and the Vatts was left filled and a quantity of half finished leather was spoiled, likewise a large quantity of raw hides collected by the farmers and of my own killing.

The same thing was [true] in every branch of business which I carried on at the time. I began to harvest my wheat, while others was digging and washing Gold, but even the Indians could not be keeped longer at Work. They was impatient to run to the mines, and other Indians had informed them of the Gold and its Value; and so I had to leave more as [than] 2/3 of my harvest in the fields.

March 21th, 1848. Threatened by a band of Robers, from the Red Woods at San Francisquito near Santa Clara.

April 2d. Mr. Humphrey a regular Miner arrived, and left for Columa with Wimmer & Marshall. Entered with them in Mining; furnished Indians, teams and provisions to this Company, and as I was loosing instead [of] making something, I left this Company as a Partner. Some of the Neighbors, while the Mormons left, became likewise [afflicted with] the Goldfever and went to the Mountains prospecting and soon afterwards moved up to digg and wash Gold, and some of them with great success.

April 16th. [Arrived] Mr. Gray (from Virginia) who [had] purchased Silver [quicksilver] Mines in the San José Valley for a Compy and was interested himself. At the fort he learned of the Gold Discovery. I presented him some Speciments of Gold. He left for the States across the Mountains. Some families are moving in the Mountains to camp and settle there.

April 18th. More curious people arrived, bound for the Mountains. I left for Columa, in Company with Major P. B. Reading and Mr. Kembel (Editor of the Alta-California) we were absent 4 Days. We was prospecting and found Silver and iron or[e] in abundance.

April 28th. A great many people more went up to the Mountains. This day the Saw mill was in Operation and the first Lumber has been sawed in the whole upper Country.

May 1th. Saml Brannan was building a store at Natoma, Mormon Islands, and have done a very large and heavy business.

May 15th. Paid off all the Mormons which has been employed by me, in building these Mills and other Mechanical trades, all of them made their pile, and some of them became rich & wealthy, but all of them was bound to the great Salt Lake, and spent there their fortunes to the honor and Glory of the Lord!

May 19th. The great Rush from San Francisco arrived at the fort, all my friends and acquaintances filled up the houses and the whole fort, I had only a little Indian boy, to make them roasted Ripps etc. as my Cooks left me like every body else. The Merchants, Doctors, Lawyers, Sea Captains, Merchants etc. all came up and did not know what to do, all was in a Confusion, all left their wives and families in San francisco, and those which had none locked their Doors, abandoned their houses, offered them for sale cheap, a few hundred Dollars House & Lot (Lots which are worth now $100,000, and more), some of these men were just like greazy [crazy].

Some of the Merchants has been the most prudentest of the Whole, visited the Mines and returned immediately and began to do a very profitable business, and soon Vessels came from every where with all Kind of Merchandise, the whole old thrash [trash] which was laying for Years unsold, on the Coasts of South & Central America, Mexico, Sandwich Islands etc. All found a good Market here.

Mr. Brannan was erecting a very large Warehouse, and have done an immense business, connected with Howard & Green; S. Francisco.

May 21th. Saml Kyburg [Kyburz] errected or established the first Hotel in the fort in the larger building, and made a great deal of Money. A great Many traders deposited a great deal of goods in my Store (an Indian was the Key Keeper and performed very well). Afterwards every little Shanty became a Warehouse and Store; the fort was then a veritable Bazaar. As white people would not be employed at the Time I had a few good Indians attending to the Ferry boat, and every night [they] came up, and delivered the received Money for ferryage to me, after deduction for a few bottles of brandy, for the whole of them. Perhaps some white people at the time would not have acted so honestly.

May 25th. The travelling to the Mines was increasing from day to day, and no more Notice was taken, as the people arrived from South America, Mexico, Sandwich Islands, Oregon etc. All the Ships Crews, and Soldiers deserted. In the beginning of July, [arrived] Col. Mason our Military Governor, with Capt. Sherman (Secretary of State) Capt. Folsom, Quartermstr, and an Escort of which some deserted, and some other Gentlemen, travelled in Company with the Governor.

As we wanted to celebrate the 4th of July we invited the Governor and his suite to remain with us, and he accepted. Kyburg gave us a good Diner, every thing was pretty well arranged. Pinkett [Pickett] was the Orator. It was well done enough for such a new Country and in such an excitement and Confusion.

And from this time on you know how every thing was going on here. One thing is certain that the people looked on my property as their own, and in the Winter of 1849 to 1850. A great Number of horses has been stolen from me, whole Manadas of Mares driven away and taken to Oregon etc. Nearly my whole Stock of Cattle has been Killed, several thousands, and left me a very small Quantity. The same has been done with my large stock of Hogs, which was running like ever under nobodies care and so it was easy to steal them. I had not an Idea that people could be so mean, and that they would do a Wholesale business in Stealing.

On the upper Sacramento, that is, from the [Sutter] Buttes downward to the point or Mouth of feather River, there was most all of my Stock running and during the Overflow the Cattle was in a many bands on high spots like Islands. There was a fine chance to approach them in small Boats and shoot them. This business has been very successfully done by one party of 5 Men (partners) which had besides hired people, and Boats Crew's, which transported the beef to the Market at Sacramento City and furnished that City with my own beef, and because these Men was nearly alone, on account of the Overflow, and Monopolized the Market.

In the Spring of 1850, these 5 men divided their Spoil of $60,000 clear profits made of Cattle. All of them left for the Atlantic State[s]; one of them returned again in the Winter from 1850 to 51, hired a new band of Robers to follow the same business and kill of[f] the balance or the few that was left. My Bacqueros found out this Nest of thiefs in their Camp butchering just some heads of my Cattle. On their return they informed me what they have seen. In the neighborhood of the same Camp they saw some more cows shot dead, which the Rascal then butchered. Immediately I did send to Nicolaus for the Sheriff (Jas. Hopkins) as then at the time we had laws in force?!? After all was stolen and destroyed the Sheriff arrived at Hock farm. I furnished him a Posse of my employed Men. They proceeded over on the Sacramento to where the thiefs were encamped. As the Sheriff wanted to arrest them they just jumped in their Boats and off they went, the Sheriff threatened them to fire at them, but they was all [armed?], and laughing they went at large.

One day my Son was riding after Stock a few miles below Hock farm. He found a Man (his name was Owens) butchering one of our finest milch Cows (of Durham stock of Chile, which cost $300). He told the Man that he could not take the Meat, that he would go home and get people, and so he has done, and he got people and a Wagon and returned to the Spot, but Owens found it good to clear out. Two brothers of this Man was respectable Merchants in Lexington Mo. and afterwards in Westport well acquainted with me. He came one day in my house and brought me their compliments, I received him well, and afterwards [he] turned out to be a thief. How many of this kind came to California which loosed their little honor by crossing the Istmus or the plains.

I had nothing at all to do with speculations, but stuck by the plough, but by paying such high Wages, and particularly under Kyburg' management, I have done this business with a heavy loss as the produce had not more the Value like before, and from the time on [after] Kyburg left I curtailed my business considerable, and so far that I do all at present with my family and a few Indian Servants. I did not speculate, only occupied my land, in the hope that it [my land title claims] would be before long decided and in my favor by the U. S. Land Commission; but now already 3 years & two months have elapsed, and I am waiting now very anxiously for the Decission, which will revive [me] or bring me to the untimely grave.

All the other Circumstances you know all yourself, perhaps I have repeated many things which I wrote in the 3 first sheets, because I had them not to see what I wrote, and as it is now several months I must have forgotten. Well it is only a kind of memorandum, and not a History at all, Only to remember you on the different periods when such and such things happened.

I need not mention again, that all the Visitors has allways been hospitably received and treated. That all the sick and wounded found allways Medical Assistance, *Gratis,* as I had nearly all the time a Physician in my employ. The Assistance to the Emigrants, that is all well known. I dont need to write anything about this.

I think now from all this you can form some facts, and that you can mention how thousands and thousands made their fortunes, from this Gold Discovery produced through my industry and energy, (some wise merchants and others in San francisco called the building of this Sawmill, another of Sutter's folly) and this folly saved not only the Mercantile World from Bankruptcy, but even our General Gov't. But for me it has turned out a folly, then without having discovered the Gold, I would have become the richest wealthiest man on the Pacific Shore.

J. A. Sutter.

2

John Augustus Sutter,
Wilderness Entrepreneur

Howard R. Lamar

Beginning with his arrival in Mexican California during the summer of 1839, the Swiss émigré John Sutter attempted for nearly nine years to create a successful commercial enterprise at his fort on the lower American River. Then, soon after United States forces had conquered the region and claimed sovereignty over California, the discovery of gold at his Coloma sawmill—located far upstream on the American River's south fork—began a rush to this country that brought Sutter lasting fame and, according to his later claims, accomplished his financial ruin.

The story of Sutter and his role in California's early development has held an enduring interest for local historians and for writers who have been attracted by the singular character of this man. But we should also seek to understand the career of John Sutter in terms of its wider meanings. With this purpose, the present essay undertakes to place Sutter within the larger context of American frontier and western history. In particular, it compares the history of Sutter and his fort with the activities of other leading entrepreneurs on the frontiers of North America, adopting a perspective that helps to fix John Sutter's place firmly among a notable group of outstanding frontier figures.

Let us begin with a brief summary of the more traditional interpretations of John A. Sutter and his role in California history. As one reads the always fascinating narrative of Sutter's coming to California, his founding an "empire" near the confluence of the American and Sacramento rivers shortly thereafter, and the way the California gold rush ruined him financially, several very different and even contradictory explanations of him and his career emerge. One version argues that Sutter was an able and charming adventurer who had seen much of the world, but who despite his experience remained a naive visionary always dreaming of glory and empire. This interpretation can be found in Richard Dillon's excellent biography of Sutter, *Fool's Gold: The Decline and Fall of Captain John Sutter of California*.[1]

A recent view suggests that only by ruthless methods and strong-arm tactics toward his labor force of California Indians did he create his "empire" of New Helvetia. Albert L. Hurtado's case study of Sutter's exploitation of California Indians, presented in his *Indian Survival on the California Frontier*, leaves one persuaded that Sutter, whatever his other talents, was indeed a cruel and ruthless man.[2] On the other hand, James Peter Zollinger's well-known older biography, *Sutter: The Man and His Empire*, details all his foibles but praises him for accomplishing so much in less than eight years—a truly remarkable triumph of one man over the wilderness and its Indian inhabitants.[3]

A fourth image is that of Sutter as truly a tragic figure whose signal accomplishments were wiped out by forces beyond his control. John Bidwell, Sutter's friend and lifelong admirer, subscribed to this view.[4] Generally speaking, however, biographers have been skeptical about praising Sutter. Hubert Howe Bancroft, California's pioneer historian, had few good words to say about him, and Marguerite Eyer Wilbur pointedly entitled her biography *John Sutter: Rascal and Adventurer*.[5]

In this essay I will advance yet another interpretive approach by viewing Sutter not as a lone individual, struggling against the accidents of fate, but as one of many wilderness entrepreneurs—or empire builders—who helped shape the American West and bring its resources and promise to the attention of the world. Comparison shows, for example, that Sutter and Sutter's Fort bear a remarkable resemblance to the role and fate of William Bent and Bent's Fort on the upper Arkansas River during the 1830s and 1840s. The fortunes of New Helvetia also parallel those of John McLoughlin and Fort Vancouver, the Hudson's Bay Company outpost on the Columbia River. Likewise, the saga of Alexander Baranov's turbulent reign at New Archangel (Sitka), the capital of Russian America, brings to mind arresting similarities to the events that occurred at Sutter's Fort. Even the career of an earlier frontier entrepreneur, Sir William Johnson in colonial New York, deserves comparison with Sutter's life in California. As I hope to demonstrate, in the broader context of common patterns of frontier development, Sutter's career seems not only less unique and less tragic, but actually representative of an evolutionary political and economic process that took place all over the American West.

On the Fourth of July, 1839, California's Governor Juan Bautista de Alvarado attended in Monterey, the capital of this Mexican province, a party given by United States Consul Thomas O. Larkin. During the event he was intrigued by a pudgy, square-set, purposeful but charming and somewhat mysterious stranger named John A. Sutter.[6] Sutter impressed the governor and other guests as a Swiss gentleman seeking to settle in California.

As is well known, Sutter had sailed into Monterey on the brig *Clementine* the day before, armed with so many letters of introduction from high-ranking persons in the Pacific area that Governor Alvarado was overwhelmed. One letter came from James Douglas, then in command of Fort Vancouver for the Hudson's Bay Company. Another came from Captain Ivan Kuprianov, the elderly governor of the Russian-American Company at New Archangel, Alaska. A third came from John C. Jones, U.S. consul at Honolulu. Jones's letter described Sutter as a captain, a Swiss gentleman, and a person of the first class among men, "who goes to California with the intention of settling there if the country meets with his expectations."[7] Jones and Sutter had cleverly put the ball in Alvarado's court, so that the question was not, would Sutter qualify for California, but would California satisfy Sutter? Far more than just perfunctory letters of introduction, those Sutter presented were characterized by warmth and great praise of his character and ability.

As a natural-born entrepreneur, formerly a dry goods merchant in Switzerland and then a Santa Fé trader, Sutter was selling what was, at the time, his only asset: himself. Accompanied by some ten or so Hawaiians, two Germans, and a large bulldog acquired in Honolulu, he proposed to establish an outpost and settlement in the interior, presumably to trade with the Indians while controlling them. By so doing he would secure the frontier for California's Mexican government against the inroads of Anglo-Americans from the aggressive young

Republic that already had established its claim to all the territory west-ward to the Rocky Mountains. Moreover, he promised to develop a trade in furs that would force out the Hudson's Bay Company's fur brigades from the Oregon Country, which were exploiting the interior valley at least as far southward as the Sacramento–San Joaquin Delta area and the lower San Joaquin drainage.[8]

Like a brilliant salesman who seemed to know exactly his customers' needs, Sutter had touched on the concerns of Mexican California's officials: that is, they too were worried that the Hudson's Bay Company was taking furs from the Central Valley. They were also nervous that a second group of fur traders, the Russians at Bodega Bay and Fort Ross, might establish a strong foothold in California. In addition, Governor Alvarado was anxious to curb the ambitions and power of his young uncle and political rival, Mariano Vallejo of Sonoma, who was commander general of the northern district.[9] A new presence in the north and in the interior would be a counterpoise both to the Russians at Fort Ross and Vallejo at Sonoma. As noted by biographer James Peter Zollinger, some of Sutter's letters of recommendation were actually addressed to General Vallejo.[10] By ingratiating himself with both Alvarado and Vallejo, diplomat Sutter did not intend for anybody to be angry with him.

Sutter is said to have presented himself to Alvarado as a promoter of colonization, for Mexican California was then granting large tracts of land to colonizers or *empresarios;* but it was with the promise that they would bring in settlers. Then, after ten years, the property of the *empresarios* might be divided among the settlers. This news, Alvarado later revealed, "made Sutter rather pensive."[11]

Far from being naive about Mexican land grants, Sutter had been aware of what was going on in the way of colonizing grants and land speculation in the Mexican borderlands ever since he had arrived in America in the mid-1830s. Almost from the time of his arrival, Sutter had been living in Missouri. There he came to know recent German immigrants, among whom there were great debates about where to settle in the Mississippi Valley. One set of vigorous propagandists argued that the Mexican province of Texas, in which Missourian Stephen F. Austin had founded a successful colony as an *empresario de colonización,* was the best place.[12] Eventually so many German colonists came to Texas that they constituted one-seventh of the early population. Even if the precedent did not impress itself on Sutter, it was hard to ignore the fact that in 1835–36 the Anglo-Americans in Texas had successfully rebelled against the Mexican authorities and established their own Texas Republic.

But it is also the case that while Sutter lived in Missouri, he became a Santa Fé trader and traveled to New Mexico for two seasons during the mid-1830s. New Mexico at that time was full of shrewd Missouri traders like Charles and William Bent, Ceran St. Vrain, and Charles Beaubien. The latter two men eventually acquired huge land grants in that province. In 1833, only two years before Sutter made his first trip to Santa Fé, Charles Bent and Ceran St. Vrain had constructed Bent's Fort, to be managed by Charles's brother William. The younger Bent's presence and influence was so powerful that almost inevitably Bent's Fort soon came to be called Fort William. Built on the north bank of the Arkansas River twelve miles upstream from the confluence of the Arkansas and the Purgatoire, it was "strategically located on the north-south trade axis between the Platte River drainage and Sante Fe and on the east-west route of the Sante Fe Trail."[13] In a remarkably short time this establishment became "a center for Indian trade, the collecting of furs and buffalo robes, stock raising and other enterprises." Bent's Fort was, in fact, to become one of the most famous multipurpose trading posts in the whole American West, and its owners, the Bent brothers and Ceran St. Vrain, were men well known to Mexicans and Anglo-Americans alike.[14]

It would probably be an insult to the ambitious young Sutter's intelligence to think that he was not aware of the incredible commercial success of the Bents with their fort, and with their trading and land connections in Santa Fé and Taos. In short, operations at Bent's Fort undoubtedly offered a model for a future Sutter's Fort.[15]

The circumstantial evidence that Sutter entertained such ideas is strengthened by the fact that he befriended Charles Beaubien, a French Canadian who had been a fur trader in New Mexico and who then married into a Mexican family and received a large land grant. A naturalized citizen, Beaubien served as alcalde of Taos, a position roughly equivalent to a justice of the peace, and later as a United States territorial judge in New Mexico. Not only did Sutter and Beaubien become friends while the former was in Taos in the 1830s, but Beaubien had also been to California as a youth and described the country and its delightful climate to Sutter in flattering terms. According to Zollinger, Sutter later said that Beaubien's tales had persuaded him that he must see this wonderful place called California.[16]

Again it seems inconceivable that Beaubien and Sutter, sitting in Taos, New Mexico, would have discussed only California's landscape and climate. Surely they also spoke of the land grants that could be acquired there. One wonders whether Sutter did not also discuss California's Indian population, which Beaubien might have compared to the peaceful Puebloans of New Mexico. In short, while some of Sutter's biographers have presented the image of Sutter as depressed or even suicidal, as a failure in business and deeply in debt to Missouri friends, it seems more likely that when he set out overland for California in the 1830s, he was then envisioning a hopeful future in a new Spanish borderland region, said to be far more fertile, more promising, and less exploited than New Mexico.[17]

No person bent on suicide would have promoted himself as an ex-captain of the Royal Swiss Guard of King Charles X of France, the convenient fiction that Sutter circulated about himself while still in Missouri and often repeated in later years. Nor does a suicidal person take along a Mexican mule driver, Pablo Gutiérrez from Santa Fé, or an Indian boy, purchased halfway across the continent, as a guide. Nor would a man considering self-destruction take in tow along the way two fellow Europeans, Niklaus Allgeier, a Bavarian, and Sebastian Keyser from the Tyrol.[18] His overland trek was a speculative venture, not a suicidal flight.

Sutter went west in a large and diverse company. The leader was Andrew Drips, a veteran American Fur Company trader who was freighting trade goods to the annual fur rendezvous taking place that season at the confluence of the Popo Agie and Wind rivers in modern Wyoming. Captain William Drummond Stewart, a wealthy son of a Scottish nobleman and a sportsman—who a year before had hired Alfred Jacob Miller to paint western scenes as a record of his adventures in the wilds of western North America—was another interesting and, for Sutter, informative member of the expedition. As was always the case when he met someone of importance, Sutter extracted a letter of recommendation from Captain Stewart.[19] In addition, the party included a band of Oregon-bound Congregational missionaries and their wives, led by the self-important and quarrelsome William Gray, who was able to add to Sutter's knowledge of conditions in the Columbia River region.

Bernard DeVoto suggests that on the Oregon Trail, Sutter and the Drips party may have met Joseph Walker, who was taking east a herd of California horses, intending to sell them at the fur-trading posts on the plains. As one of the first Anglo-Americans to find an overland route to California, Walker surely would have told Sutter something about California. Indeed, Joe Walker had spent the winter of 1833–34 in the Sacramento–San Joaquin Valley, where Sutter eventually located.[20]

As luck would have it, one Captain Francis Ermatinger, a Canadian of Swiss ancestry who worked for the Hudson's Bay Company, was at the American fur trade rendezvous in 1838. Ermatinger helped Sutter and his party to reach Fort Hall and then provided a guide to get them to Fort Boise. On this part of the trip, Sutter also met Jason Lee, the pioneer Methodist missionary in the Willamette Valley who was heading east to raise money and fresh recruits for his mission enterprise at Salem.[21]

If Sutter learned more about California on the Oregon Trail, his education did not stop there. In Oregon he first visited Lee's mission establishment, by now a center of Anglo-American settlement. Soon Sutter was telling in Oregon the story that he "was on his way to California to buy cattle for Oregon, intending to leave them here"; then he would go to Switzerland, return with his family, and found a Swiss settlement. Since the Willamette Valley settlers were still badly in need of cattle, salesman Sutter was telling them what they wanted to hear. Only a year before, Ewing Young, aided by Lieutenant W. A. Slacum, had brought seven hundred head from California to the Willamette Valley.[22]

Sutter, as we know, then embarked on an introductory tour of Pacific Coast maritime trade centers. First he visited James Douglas, the acting chief factor at the Hudson's Bay Company's impressive Fort Vancouver. Douglas was so taken with Sutter that he secured passage for him and his companions on a vessel going to Honolulu, with the idea that Sutter would go from there to California. Once he arrived in Hawaii, Sutter charmed the local consuls and resident Anglo-Americans almost out of their minds before arranging a voyage to New Archangel, Alaska, as the best way of getting to California. At New

Archangel, as suggested earlier, he ingratiated himself with Captain Kuprianov, governor of the Russian-American Company, and his wife, Princess Menchnikov—impressing all by speaking in Spanish to some, in German to others, and in French to still others.[23]

The point of this lengthy recital is not to list Sutter's social conquests but to summarize his acquisition of knowledge about the various trading systems that operated along the Pacific Coast. By the time Sutter reached California he had personally witnessed how the three most successful trading posts in the entire West worked: Bent's Fort, Fort Vancouver, and the Russian headquarters at New Archangel. (On his way west he had also visited Fort Laramie, an important enterprise for the American Fur Company.) He knew what they traded and what they needed. He could see that two were located near the confluence of two rivers: Bent's Fort on the Arkansas upstream from the Purgatoire, and Fort Vancouver on the Columbia near the mouth of the Willamette. Bent's Fort and Fort Vancouver were also situated on established trade routes, while Fort Vancouver and New Archangel had access to the Pacific Ocean. He also must have realized that New Archangel was vulnerable due to the fact that it had no adequate local food supply, depending on wheat and other foodstuffs imported from Fort Ross, its California outpost.

In choosing to locate near the confluence of the American and the Sacramento rivers, John Sutter combined a frontier trading-outpost concept with the idea of maritime trade in a spot where fur traders moved back and forth from the Oregon Country to California's Central Valley, and where Anglo-Americans would naturally gather after an overland trek across the Sierra Nevada.[24] In terms of crash-course preparation, Sutter was as well versed as any trader ever needed to be in order to establish a successful outpost in the wilderness. Moreover, Albert Hurtado indicates that Sutter also adopted the Indian labor system practiced at the California missions and on the ranchos as a model for his own labor force at New Helvetia.[25] Between 1839 and 1846, when the Bear Flag Revolt occurred, Sutter's Fort grew from a set of Hawaiian-style grass huts to an adobe structure of imposing size. In some ways it resembled Bent's Fort, also built of adobe. After Sutter purchased Fort Ross, however, he hauled some of the Russian-built wood structures from the Mendocino coast to New Helvetia for in-

"From Flora's Garden." Undated view of Sutter's Fort, ca. 1858, charcoal on paper drawing by Thomas A. Ayers. Courtesy of the Society of California Pioneers and Sutter's Fort Museum, California State Dept. of Parks and Recreation.

corporation into Sutter's Fort. Just as Spanish, Russian, British, and Anglo-American fur traders had met in the Sacramento–San Joaquin Valley in the 1830s, at least symbolically a Siberian–North Pacific wood culture met an adobe culture from the Southwest in the buildings of Sutter's Fort.[26]

What Sutter tried to do to turn his wilderness outpost into an empire—a genuine New Helvetia—in seven short years is impressive by itself. As was the case at the other great outposts that he had visited, he now traded with Indians, participated in the fur trade, tried to raise food, and successfully built up herds of horses and cattle. With an energy often marked by a sense of desperation, and with reliance on Indian labor, he began to raise wheat and distill brandy from local grapes. Moreover, he tried his hand at irrigation, though he never understood that his wheat crops required it. He set out fruit trees, raised sheep, had Indian women weave woolen blankets, and tried to manufacture wool felt hats.[27]

That Sutter succeeded at all was the more impressive because he had no resources of his own. He overstretched his credit with merchants William A. Leidesdorff and Nathan Spear in Monterey and Yerba Buena for many kinds of supplies, with Mariano Vallejo for cattle, and with Anglo-Americans in the vicinity like John Marsh for cattle and articles meant for the Indian trade. Sutter soon became notorious for his unwillingness to pay bills; but somehow he managed to placate most of his creditors.

Further, as Albert Hurtado has noted, Sutter introduced various Indian groups to routines of daily work set by the European time clock and calendar. He had an Indian military contingent to defend his property and retaliate against hostiles. Almost by default he became a frontier military commander and a civilian alcalde in one. He did not hesitate to execute Indian enemies, perform wedding ceremonies, or get rid of an out-of-favor mistress by marrying her to one of his workers.[28]

But if we are to look at Sutter in entrepreneurial terms, we must also realize what he was up against. Unlike the British in the Oregon Country or the Russians in Alaska, he had no government-protected monopoly to back him up; unlike the Bents, he was not well-heeled when he began building his empire. Sutter also had enemies. Simply by establishing himself as a second authority figure in the interior valley, he became a counterpoise and therefore a threat to General Vallejo. Nor was he trusted by the Mexican authorities at Monterey. Sutter, in fact, was surrounded by potential and real adversaries and rivals: *Californios,* Indians, the Russians at Fort Ross, and even the Hudson's Bay Company, which continued to send fur brigades down to the Central Valley to compete with his own hunters.

Unlike so many entrepreneurs, Sutter did not have support from business partners or a real company structure. The Bents had St. Vrain, other friendly white traders, and even Indian allies to assist them. McLoughlin had the backing of the Hudson's Bay Company. In contrast, Sutter ran a one-man show. To be sure, Sutter's friendliness and charismatic charm attracted many able individuals to work for him, including John Bidwell, William Swasey, Heinrich Lienhard, George McKinstry, William Grimshaw, Pierson B. Reading, and later, of course, James Marshall; but these associates and boon companions formed a loosely allied retinue, frequently changing, not a business organization.[29]

In the course of erecting his empire, Sutter learned that one must have not just a labor force, but also craftsmen, artisans, suppliers, and the right tools and trade goods to succeed. Fort Vancouver and, to a lesser degree, New Archangel had skilled blacksmiths and gunsmiths, carpenters, farmers, herdsmen, and grist-mill operators. Sutter at first had none; nor could the Indians or Mexican population adequately supply these skills. John Bidwell tells of Indians having to cut wheat with iron hooks or sharp reeds. The Fort Sutter account book suggests that blacksmith Samuel Neal was in such demand that he worked night and day fashioning or repairing needed metal tools.[30]

Sutter found those missing artisans—those blacksmiths, carpenters, and the like—among the Anglo-American overland immigrants arriving in California, for whom Sutter's Fort was the first sign of civilization after crossing the Great Basin and the Sierra. Similarly he found that what few supplies he could get came from the New England expatriate John Marsh, from the Anglo-American merchant traders on the coast like Thomas O. Larkin and Nathan Spear, and from the West Indies–born William Leidesdorff. Moreover, the non-Hispanic newcomers were likely to be the main purchasers of his furs, horses, cattle, and grain.

Since Governor Alvarado had originally authorized Sutter's venture to secure California's northern interior against wild Indians and Anglo-American intrusion, the history of New Helvetia has more than a touch of irony. Sutter's Fort became the port of entry for Anglo-Americans from the eastern states as well as a trading center for Indians all the way north to Oregon and as far south as the Mariposa region. Moreover, particularly since he had resided in Missouri for some years, Sutter attracted a wide circle of associates with interests distinct from those of Hispanic Californians. Easily influenced by those around him and struggling for economic survival, the master of Sutter's Fort pointed New Helvetia toward a destiny far different from that which he and Governor Alvarado had originally intended.[31]

When Sir George Simpson, the brilliant, calculating governor-in-chief of the Hudson's Bay Company, came to California in 1841, he at once saw the larger strategic, economic, and political meaning of Sutter's Fort:

> If he [Sutter] really has the talent and courage to make the most of his position, he is not unlikely to render California a second Texas. Even now the Americans only want a rallying-point for carrying into effect their theory that the English race is destined by "right divine" to expel the Spaniards from their ancient seats, a theory which has already begun to develop itself in more ways than one. . . . Now, for fostering and maturing Brother Jonathan's ambitious views, Captain Sutter's establishment is admirably situated. Besides lying on the direct route between San Francisco on the one hand and the Missouri and Willamette on the other, it virtually excludes the Californians from all the best parts of their own country.—the valleys of the San Joaquin, the Sacramento, and the Colorado. Hitherto the Spaniards have confined themselves to the comparatively barren slip of land, varying from ten to forty miles in width, which lies between the ocean and the first range of mountains, and beyond this slip they will never penetrate with their present character and their present force, if Captain Sutter, or any other adventurer, can gather round him a score of such marksmen as won Texas on the field of San Jacinto.

In Sir George's perceptive analysis, the importance of Sutter's Fort extended well beyond the Central Valley. "For the Americans," he added, "if masters of the interior, will soon discover that they have a natural right to a maritime outlet, so that, whatever may be the fate of Monterey and the more southerly ports, San Francisco will, to a moral certainty, sooner or later fall into the hands of the Americans. . . ."[32] In other words, Sir George believed that Sutter's Fort was the key not just to the Central Valley, but to future control over San Francisco Bay as well, potentially the most significant commercial and military site along the entire Pacific Coast of North America.

When Sutter bought Fort Ross from the Russians in 1841, he so overextended himself financially that he may well have ruined his chances for keeping his empire, even without a Bear Flag Revolt in 1846 or the discovery of gold in January of 1848. Yet what he accomplished in the eight and a half years between his arrival and the beginning of the gold rush was phenomenal. At first he could supply only furs, hides, captive or rented Indian labor, and grape brandy; but by 1846 he was selling wheat and cattle, his tannery produced leather for shoes and saddles, his blacksmiths were making spurs and bridle bits, and local Indian women wove blankets and felted hats from the wool supplied by his flocks of sheep.

The New Helvetia Diary of 1845–48, kept by Sutter, Bidwell, Swasey, and Loker, records that Sutter's establishment supplied thirty sides of sole leather for Don Miguel Pedrorena, twenty-nine sides for John C. Davis, and another ten sides of upper leather for John Williams. From his growing flocks, Sutter delivered a hundred sheep to William Leidesdorff. Samuel Neal, one of Sutter's blacksmiths in 1845, was busy making cranks, augers, and hinges.[33] The Hawaiians who had accompanied Sutter to the Sacramento Valley raised hogs and built him a hog pen. When John C. Frémont arrived in 1845 and peremptorily demanded horses and mules, Sutter's agents toured the local ranches to find them.

At the same time, the New Helvetia Diary also suggests that Sutter's employees were constantly making do. In October and November of 1847, for example, the record says they were turning a barracks into a warehouse for wheat and using bricks from a barracks chimney to make a "new fire" in the blacksmith shop.[34]

Concerning the Bear Flag Revolt and the U.S. conquest of California, much has been made of how Frémont humiliated Sutter by placing young Lieutenant Edward Kern in charge of Sutter's Fort. But Sutter, now a lieutenant himself, had fifty enlisted men under him, and he saw to it that they got clothes, rations, and pay from the United States government, with himself getting a bigger share than the others.[35] Indeed, Sutter's Fort appears to have played a larger role in outfitting and provisioning the Anglo-American conquerors than we realize. Besides providing horses, mules, tools, and foodstuffs for Frémont, New Helvetia's fields and workshops supplied food and goods to the U.S. naval ships on the coast. On the other hand, the rudimentary nature of New Helvetia's commercial operations in 1846 can be seen in the Sutter's Fort record of Edward Kern, who tried to order silk handkerchiefs, saleratus, raisins, and braid, along with tea, sugar, and coffee, from coastal merchants. Most of these items Kern found simply were not available at the fort, while others were prohibitively expensive.[36] The Sutter's Fort trade, however limited, was a two-way traffic.

Sutter claimed later that he had prospered in 1846–47, at the time of the Anglo-American conquest of California, and declared that he would have continued to do so but for epidemics among Indian workers and, of course, the consequences of an event noted in the New Helvetia Diary for July 21, 1847: "Marshall with Nerio left to the Mountains on the Amer: fork, to select the site for the Saw Mill." Then a few months later came another entry: "Mr. Marshall arrived from the Mountains on very important business."[37]

It could be argued that Sutter was only the last and most dramatic of a familiar type of frontier entrepreneur who helped develop North America. The number of organizations that they managed was truly impressive, ranging from colonial Indian and fur-trading outposts to the big companies like those of the Chouteaus and the American and Rocky Mountain fur firms that operated out of St. Louis during the nineteenth century. But the roll of wilderness entrepreneurs should also include colonizers such as Stephen F. Austin in Texas and Brigham Young in Utah, as well as smaller on-site traders such as the Torrey brothers in Texas.[38] To be sure, all of them failed; but by failing in their original purpose they succeeded in accomplishing a larger one. Several examples help illustrate this generalization.

Let us go back to exactly one hundred years before John Sutter set out from Missouri in 1838 to seek his destiny in California. In 1738 a young Irishman named William Johnson came to America and settled in the frontier area of New York Province. He located on the south side of the Mohawk River near the mouth of the Schoharie. Although he had migrated initially to manage an estate belonging to an uncle, Admiral Sir Peter Warren, Johnson went immediately into the fur trade, selling goods to Indians and nearby white settlers alike. In 1739, a hundred years before Sutter settled in the Sacramento Valley, Johnson got a tract of land near present-day Amsterdam, New York. An ambitious, land-hungry man, he built up one of the largest landed estates in British colonial America.[39] He befriended the Six Nations of the Iroquois, married an Indian woman—after his German-born wife had died—and then, after the death of his second wife, married Molly Brant, sister of the powerful Iroquois leader Joseph Brant. Johnson was a wonderful diplomat, a fine trader, and a crucial figure in Indian affairs. One has to say he was a far more organized and able entrepreneur than John Sutter ever was. As a "Colonel of the Six Nations" and a baronet, Sir William Johnson's titles were more legitimate than Sutter's self-promotion to be captain of the Swiss Guards and general of a California regiment.

Johnson lived in style at Johnson Hall like a nobleman, much as Sutter wanted to live and perhaps did for a brief time at Hock Farm. Yet as one of Johnson's biographers has noted, "He did not foresee the rapidity with which conditions were to be changed by the westward march of the white settlers, but rather to have visualized a static condition with a boundary line holding back the tide of settlement."[40] By opening up the Mohawk Valley, Johnson sowed the seeds of his own destruction. Although he died on the eve of the American Revolution, his son, Sir John Johnson, and his son-in-law, Sir Guy Johnson, lost their estates because they were Tories. Sir Guy spent his last years in London trying to secure compensation from Parliament for the loss of his estates, much like Sutter's attempts, a century later, to persuade Congress to pay him for his lost lands.[41]

In similar fashion, William Bent saw his trading empire and his success at maintaining peaceful Indian relations on the Arkansas ruined by gold seekers on their way to Pike's Peak in Colorado in 1859. He tried to sell his fort to the U.S. government, just as Sutter tried to sell his post to the army; but when the U.S. offered an insultingly low price, Bent blew up the structure and built another elsewhere. A sense of loyalty to their Cheyenne mother and her people persuaded some of

Bent's children to become "Indian" while others declared themselves to be "white." But the point is that the westward march of Anglo-American settlers ruined Bent's empire, just as it had Johnson's and Sutter's.[42]

In far away Oregon, Dr. John McLoughlin, the Hudson's Bay Company's chief factor at Fort Vancouver, for many years ran a small empire based on furs, trade goods, cattle, farm produce, salmon fishing, and timber. He successfully held back Anglo-American fur trappers by pursuing a scorched-earth policy for twenty years, trapping out the interior just as Sutter was supposed to do to Hudson's Bay trapping territory in the San Joaquin Valley.[43] But, inevitably, Anglo-American settlers came. McLoughlin, rather than trying to freeze them out, greeted them, fed them, and supplied them with all the warmth and openness characteristic of Sutter's hospitality toward trail-weary emigrants from the Mississippi Valley. But McLoughlin also realized that the fur trade was declining and that Oregon might become part of the United States. He invested in property at a mill site in Oregon City, only to lose his estate because he was not a naturalized U.S. citizen, and because of the jealousy of other land-hungry settlers. He and his devoted part-Indian wife eked out a modest existence in Oregon City for the rest of their lives, much as Sutter and his wife were to do in a small Pennsylvania town during their last years. McLoughlin, beset by legal fees and defeat in the U.S. courts, could compare his lot to that of Sutter, Sir Guy Johnson, and William Bent.[44]

Yet there is another side to this story. Hudson's Bay Company officials such as Sir George Simpson and James Douglas had long understood that Oregon furs were playing out, and that Anglo-American settlers would take over before long. Secretly, they undermined McLoughlin's sincere efforts to "hold the fort," as it were, planning to withdraw to Vancouver Island and establish a new headquarters at Victoria. With the Americanization of Oregon south of the Columbia River by settlers, followed by the signing of the Oregon Boundary Treaty in 1846, the Hudson's Bay Company did just that. James Douglas, whom Sutter had visited in 1838 at Fort Vancouver on the Columbia, closed out operations at Fort Vancouver and founded Fort Victoria in 1849.

But for Sir George Simpson and other company officials, this would be the last retreat from the Anglo-Americans. When a Hudson's Bay Company employee discovered gold on Canada's Fraser River in 1858, California's placer gold was playing out, and so some 25,000 miners, mostly from California, took boats to Victoria and went on to the Fraser River, or else they came up the Columbia River to the Fraser. Douglas saw Anglo-American merchants taking over Victoria. What had been a town of three hundred was soon a little city of several thousand, of whom nine-tenths were Anglo-Americans or Europeans. Douglas believed that if he did not take action, the next step would be for the Anglo-Americans to take over the region by the process of popular sovereignty, miners' courts, and self-government.

To prevent such an outcome, in 1858 the British Parliament created the colony of British Columbia and made Douglas its governor. He, in turn, appointed gold commissioners to run the camps, and the British government designated a tall, powerful, ruthless judge, Matthew Baille Begbie, to exact justice. Judge Begbie became a kind of Stephen J. Field for the Canadian Far West. Faced by the determined wills and policies of Douglas and Begbie, the Americans behaved.[45] The British policy of holding back the Anglo-Americans was aided by the fact that the Fraser River mines had many shortcomings: the season was short, the distance long, and the mining areas remote; and so the boom soon ended. Most Anglo-Americans quickly went back to the States or moved on to new gold strikes in the American Rockies.

When a second gold rush to the Cariboo region occurred in the 1860s, the British were ready for that one, too, and it remained largely a British frontier. British royal engineers provided protection for the gold-seekers and built vital links to the gold fields as well. But when an American outlaw named Ned McGowan tried to take over a town and commit robberies, government troops descended in such force that Americans knew it was no contest.[46] To be sure, Victoria soon became a regular settlement instead of a fur trade capital; but unlike all the other fur-trading enterprises in the West, which eventually failed or closed up shop, the Hudson's Bay Company survived by going into general trade and continuing to serve relatively unpopulated areas. The company's survival is, in fact, an exception to the generalization that wilderness empires fulfill their ultimate destiny by failing.

To the north, in Russian Alaska, the fur business was also in decline; indeed, the Russian-American Company ships were now more engaged in the China tea trade than in furs. And while no population rush to Alaska ever overwhelmed this imperial outpost, eventually Russia decided to sell Alaska to the United States, an act that averted what might have been a British or American takeover.[47] These trading empires created the favorable conditions that led settlers to come and fur supplies to decline, thus hastening the empire's demise. In that long progress of frontier commercial ventures from the Virginia Company to Sir William Johnson in New York, to the Panton Leslie Company in British Florida, to Bent's Fort at the edge of the Colorado Rockies and the Chouteaus on the Oklahoma plains to Fort Vancouver, and finally to Sutter's Fort and New Archangel, we see a process in which wilderness entrepreneurs like John Sutter were absolutely essential—but destined to fail. In short, John Sutter had played out his role successfully by 1846. The Bear Flag Rebellion and gold rush were not his climactic years, but an aftermath.

John Sutter was often foolish, impulsive, impolitic, needlessly cruel to Indians, and temperamental. He was outrageous in his behavior to his own son, who had more business sense than he did.[48] These qualities helped destroy what estate he did have after the gold rush; but in the perspective of time, one man—not a company or a government-protected monopoly—opened the way for American settlers in California. That is no mean achievement for the short, fat, charming adventurer from Burgdorf. Like others of his kind, by sowing the seeds of his own ruin this most charming of these wilderness entrepreneurs succeeded in history beyond his wildest dreams.

After the death of John Augustus Sutter in 1880, John Bidwell, his one-time clerk, surveyor, and assistant who had helped keep the New Helvetia Diary from 1845 to 1848, wrote to William F. Swasey, who formerly was one of Sutter's clerks. Bidwell's letter contained a fitting epitaph: "Marshall may have discovered the gold," he wrote, "but in a broader and grander sense—in a great and true sense—Sutter was the discoverer." The "great discovery" he continued, ". . . awakened our country into new life—Its wonderful power moved the world, and led not only to a mass migration of people, but to the discovery of silver in Nevada, gold in Australia and gave the Union the resources to fight the Civil War."

Bidwell's Sutter was "under Providence the humble instrument or forerunner . . . who had a large business capacity. . . . But his hope in the future always led him to undertake too much." Bidwell then added, "It seems almost a mockery to starve the noble pioneer to death, and starve his broken hearted wife to death also, and then immediately proceed to do grand things to perpetuate his memory."[49] But one must distinguish between process and high tragedy. Sutter, though a brilliant wilderness entrepreneur, was but part of a larger, almost inevitable process.

Let us give Sutter's old friend George McKinstry the last word. Writing in 1851 to Edward Kern, who was back East, he said:

> The 'Embarcadero' is now the large city of Sacramento, the old fort is fast going to decay; the last time I was there I rode through and there was not a living soul to be seen. What a fall is there, my fellow. . . . Times are not as they uster was.

But McKinstry felt Sutter was doing well at Hock Farm; Sam Neal, the Sutter's Fort blacksmith, was prospering as a farmer, and though many pioneers had boomed and busted, McKinstry said California was doing well. Poking fun at the inclination of Californians to boast about their state, he told Kern that cabbages there weighed fifty-three pounds per head and Irish potatoes were thirty-three inches in circumference. Cabbages and potatoes had replaced grand pioneer days, but McKinstry's mood was nostalgic rather than tragic.[50]

Whether we think of California's foremost wilderness entrepreneur as a hero, charlatan, or tragic figure, he deserves recognition and study because he borrowed and combined many ideas, techniques, economies, and cultures from other outposts of empire to use at Sutter's Fort. As we praise the way American pioneers of the colonial period survived, we should remember that they did so in part by adopting the Swedish log cabin and by using a new-style rifle that German gunsmiths perfected in Lancaster, Pennsylvania. We praise the accomplishments of American mountain men in the fur trade, but their enterprise was built on French, English, and Russian precedents. Nothing is so American as cattle ranching and cowboys, but we now know that the open-range cattle business was an amalgam of several Spanish, Mexican, and Scottish traditions and techniques.[51]

Sutter, a Swiss émigré, combined frontier commercial systems borrowed from so many others that he, too, began to look American. Because of his enterprise in shaping a successful eclectic combination, representing a larger American tradition of borrowing and adapting, we can rightly pay tribute to him as one of the great wilderness entrepreneurs.

Notes

1. Richard Dillon, *Fool's Gold: The Decline and Fall of Captain John Sutter of California* (New York: Coward-McCann, 1967; reprint, Santa Cruz, California: Western Tanager, 1981).

2. Albert L. Hurtado, *Indian Survival on the California Frontier* (New Haven: Yale University Press, 1988), pp. 55–71.

3. James Peter Zollinger, *Sutter: The Man and His Empire* (New York: Oxford University Press, 1939).

4. Book Club of California, *Pioneers of the Sacramento: A Group of Letters by and about Johann Augustus Sutter, James W. Marshall, and John Bidwell* (San Francisco: Book Club of California, 1953). See especially John Bidwell to Captain W. F. Swasey, March 12, 1881, pp. 28–30. According to Zollinger, *Sutter,* pp. 279–80, Peter H. Burnett also saw Sutter as a victim. The Sutter entry by W. J. Ghent in Allen Johnson and Dumas Malone, eds., *Dictionary of American Biography,* 20 vols. (New York: Charles Scribner's Sons, 1928–37), 18:224–25, is highly favorable, as is Julian Dana's *Sutter of California* (New York: Press of the Pioneers, 1934).

5. Hubert Howe Bancroft, *History of California,* 7 vols. (San Francisco: History Company, 1884–90); see especially 5:738–40. See also Marguerite Eyer Wilbur, *John Sutter: Rascal and Adventurer* (New York: Liveright Publishing Corporation, 1949), which is a biography full of imagined conversation, as is Dana's *Sutter of California.*

6. Zollinger, *Sutter,* pp. 54–56.

7. See Zollinger, *Sutter,* p. 54, for the text of Jones's letter.

8. Dillon, *Fool's Gold,* pp. 76–77, notes Alvarado's response to Sutter's proposal to hold off Indians, Russians, Anglo-Americans, and the British by settling in the interior. In conveying his approval of the New Helvetia grant a year later, Alvarado asserted that Sutter had "already, in advance, manifested his great efforts, his constant firmness, and truly patriotic zeal in favor of our institutions, by reducing to civilization a quantity of savage Indians, natives of

these frontiers. . . ." See John Plumbe, *A Faithful Translation of the Papers Respecting the Grant Made by Governor Alvarado to John A. Sutter* (Sacramento: Placer Times, 1850; reprint, Sacramento: Sacramento Book Collectors Club, 1942). For the Hudson's Bay Company's presence in the Central Valley, beginning with an expedition led by Peter Skene Ogden in 1829–30, see Gloria Griffin Cline, *Peter Skene Ogden and the Hudson's Bay Company* (Norman: University of Oklahoma Press, 1974), pp. 93–96; and John S. Galbraith, "A Note on the British Fur Trade in California, 1821–1846," *Pacific Historical Review* 24 (May 1955): 253–60.

9. Oscar Lewis, *Sutter's Fort: Gateway to the Gold Fields* (Englewood Cliffs, New Jersey: Prentice-Hall, 1966), p. 28.

10. Zollinger, *Sutter,* p. 54.

11. Zollinger, *Sutter,* p. 55.

12. Dillon, *Fool's Gold,* p. 27, states that Sutter was influenced by Gottfried Duden, a Swiss writer who described America in romantic terms in his *Bericht über eine Reise nach den westlichen Vereinigten Staaten* (1832).

13. David Lavender, *Bent's Fort* (Garden City, New York: Doubleday and Company, 1954), pp. 131–40, 385–86.

14. Besides full coverage of their careers in Lavender, *Bent's Fort,* brief biographies of the Bents and St. Vrain by Gordon B. Dodds appear in Howard R. Lamar, ed., *The Reader's Encyclopedia of the American West* (New York: Thomas Y. Crowell Company, 1977), pp. 87–88, 1060–61. For fuller accounts see the entries in LeRoy R. Hafen, ed., *The Mountain Men and the Fur Trade of the Far West: Biographical Sketches of the Participants by Scholars of the Subject and with Introductions by the Editor,* 10 vols. (Glendale, California: The Arthur H. Clark Co., 1965–72): s.v. "Charles Bent" and "Ceran St. Vrain" by Harold H. Dunham, 2:27–48, 5:297–316; and s.v. "George Bent" by Harvey L. Carter, 4:39–43.

15. Dillon, *Fool's Gold,* pp. 29–42, details Sutter's activities in the Santa Fé trade.

16. Dillon, *Fool's Gold,* p. 42.

17. Richard Dillon has reached a similar conclusion, remarking that "Sutter was hardly the suicidal type"; see *Fool's Gold,* p. 42.

18. Dillon, *Fool's Gold,* p. 55.

19. Dillon, *Fool's Gold,* pp. 45–46; see also Bernard DeVoto, *Across the Wide*

Missouri (Boston: Houghton Mifflin, 1947), pp. 350–51. Stewart's western years are fully described in Mae Reed Porter and Odessa Davenport, *Scotsman in Buckskin: Sir William Drummond Stewart and the Rocky Mountain Fur Trade* (New York: Hastings House, 1963). For his role as the patron of Alfred Jacob Miller, see Ron Tyler, ed., *Alfred Jacob Miller: Artist on the Oregon Trail* (Fort Worth, Texas: Amon Carter Museum, 1982).

20. DeVoto, *Across the Wide Missouri,* pp. 343, 372, 448. Walker's long and interesting career is fully recounted in Bil Gilbert, *Westering Man: The Life of Joseph Walker, Master of the Frontier* (New York: Atheneum, 1983). Although Gilbert does not mention this 1838 meeting between Walker and Sutter, he does remark that Joel Walker, the older brother of the mountain man, in 1841 briefly became the manager of Sutter's farm; see p. 178.

21. DeVoto, *Across the Wide Missouri,* pp. 358, 367, 369.

22. Dillon, *Fool's Gold,* pp. 56–57, 67; and Howard R. Lamar, "Ewing Young," in Lamar, *Reader's Encyclopedia,* pp. 1300–1301.

23. Dillon, *Fool's Gold,* p. 72; and Zollinger, *Sutter,* p. 48.

24. In a brief biographical sketch of John Sutter, historian Walton Bean has emphasized that Sutter's Fort soon became "a focal point for the increasing flow of covered wagons bringing settlers from the United States"; see Lamar, *Reader's Encyclopedia,* p. 1152. As Bean relates, Sutter welcomed these newcomers and later remarked: "They were of my breed and they loved the promise of the soil."

25. Hurtado, *Indian Survival,* p. 55.

26. Sutter's purchase of Fort Ross is noted in Zollinger, Sutter, pp. 96–97, and in Lewis, *Sutter's Fort,* pp. 39–49, 54–57.

27. The range of business activities at Sutter's Fort is demonstrated in notations throughout John A. Sutter et al., *New Helvetia Diary: A Record of Events Kept by John A. Sutter and His Clerks at New Helvetia, California, from September 9, 1845, to May 25, 1848* (San Francisco: Grabhorn Press, 1939). See especially pp. ix–xi, xxiv–xxv.

28. Hurtado, *Indian Survival,* pp. 56–59; and Dillon, *Fool's Gold,* p. 112.

29. The *New Helvetia Diary* suggests how busy these men were when they worked for Sutter. See especially entries for 1845 and 1846, with daily arrivals of traders and settlers, launches going back and forth to Yerba Buena, and Sutter sending Indian youths to work for Leidesdorff and Antonio Suñol.

30. *New Helvetia Diary* entries for late November and December, 1845, pp. 14–18, note the activities of blacksmith Samuel Neal. Entries from December 15, 1845, to February 1, 1846, pp. 18–25, also record the work of two other blacksmiths, Sanders and Kamp, who had accompanied the Frémont expedition.

31. It did not take Sutter long to decide that his future lay with American immigrants; he then sent Caleb Greenwood east to Fort Hall to urge those on the way to Oregon to come to California instead. See Charles Kelly and Dale Morgan, *The Story of Caleb Greenwood—Trapper, Pathfinder and Early Pioneer* (Georgetown, California: Talisman Press, 1965).

32. Sir George Simpson, *Narrative of a Voyage to California Ports in 1841–42, Together with Voyages to Sitka, the Sandwich Islands & Okhotsk . . . from the Narrative of a Voyage round the World*, ed. Thomas C. Russell (San Francisco: Private Press of Thomas C. Russell, 1930), pp. 73–74. Sir George did see one possible strategic alternative: if Great Britain would occupy San Francisco Bay, the United States would be preempted from assuming a dominant role. But, he concluded, "English, in some sense or other of the word, the richest portions of California must become. Either Great Britain will introduce her well-regulated freedom of all classes and colors or the people of the United States will inundate the country with their own peculiar mixture of helpless bondage and lawless insubordination. Between two such alternatives the Californians themselves have little room for choice. . . ."

33. Sutter et al., *New Helvetia Diary*, pp. 16, 19, 25, 30, 46, 47, 56–57.

34. Sutter et al., *New Helvetia Diary*, pp. 90, 91. The barracks structure, identified locally as Sutter's east adobe, served many different purposes during its short life, ending as a brewery before its collapse in 1854. For its history and subsequent use of the site, see Marvin Brienes, "East of Sutter's Fort: Block K-L-28-29 in Sacramento, 1840–1955" (Report prepared for Sutter Community Hospitals, 1983; on file, Sacramento City Planning Division); and Kenneth N. Owens, principal investigator, in Peak & Associates, Inc., "Cultural Resources Report: The K-L/28-29th Streets Block" and "Final Report on Cultural Resources within the K-L-28-29 and K-L-29-30 Blocks, Sacramento, California" (Reports prepared for Sutter Community Hospitals and Sacramento City Planning Office, 1984; on file, Sacramento City and County Archives, Sacramento History and Science Division).

35. Seymour Dunbar, ed., *The Fort Sutter Papers, Together with Historical Commentaries Accompanying Them, Brought Together in One Volume for Purposes of Reference*, 39 vols. in 1 (N.p.: Edward Eberstadt, 1922), vol. 23, MS. 94: "Payroll of Garrison at Ft. Sacramento, entered by Lieut. Missroon, U.S.N." This doc-

ument states that J. A. Sutter was lieutenant and was paid $50 a month in cash and $253.65 in clothing and tobacco. The Indian members of the garrison, on the other hand, got $12.50 a month in cash and $37.50 in clothing and tobacco. (A rare publication, with only twenty copies printed, *The Fort Sutter Papers* contain full transcripts, with introductions and editorial annotations, of documents collected by Captain Edward Kern at Sutter's Fort during the period of the American military occupation. The original manuscripts are now located in the Huntington Library, San Marino, California.)

36. Dunbar, ed., *Fort Sutter Papers,* MSS. 85, 88, 91, and 93, suggests that while Sutter's Fort was receiving clothing, beef, bread, sugar, tea, tobacco, coffee, and rice from Leidesdorff and Ridley, Captain Kern purchased cattle locally to supply his men with beef. An excellent general overview appears in Neal Harlow, *California Conquered: War and Peace on the Pacific, 1846–1850* (Berkeley: University of California Press, 1982).

37. Sutter et al., *New Helvetia Diary,* July 21, 1847, p. 61, and January 28, 1848, p. 113.

38. The lesser-known Torrey's Post near Waco, Texas, is described in Howard R. Lamar, *The Trader on the American Frontier: Myth's Victim* (College Station: Texas A & M University Press, 1977), p. 13. See also Ferdinand Roemer, *Texas,* English ed. (San Antonio: Standard Printing Company, 1935), pp. 191–96; and Benjamin Butler Harris, *The Gila Trail: The Texas Argonauts and the California Gold Rush* (Norman: University of Oklahoma Press, 1960), pp. 35–37, 35n.

39. See James T. Flexner, *Mohawk Baronet: Sir William Johnson of New York* (New York: Harper, 1959).

40. Wayne E. Stevens, in Johnson and Malone, *Dictionary of American Biography,* s.v. "William Johnson," 10:124–28.

41. Stevens, in Johnson and Malone, *Dictionary of American Biography,* s.v. "Guy Johnson" and "John Johnson," 10:100 and 103–4.

42. Lavender, *Bent's Fort,* pp. 154, 311–18, 350–51, 358, 363.

43. See Richard Gill Montgomery, *The White-Headed Eagle: John McLoughlin, Builder of an Empire* (New York: Macmillan Company, 1934).

44. Montgomery, *White-Headed Eagle,* pp. 308–16.

45. Both older and more recent biographies of Sir James Douglas exist. See especially W. N. Sage, *Sir James Douglas and British Columbia* (Toronto: Univer-

sity of Toronto Press, 1971); and Margaret A. Ormsby's account in Francess G. Halpenny, ed., *Dictionary of Canadian Biography,* 12 vols. (Toronto: University of Toronto Press, 1966–90), 10:238–49.

46. The story of Americans in the Fraser River and Cariboo gold rushes is covered in Thomas William Paterson, *British Columbia: The Pioneer Years* (Langley, British Columbia: Stagecoach, 1970), pp. 59ff., 168ff.; and in J. Friesen and H. L. Ralston, eds., *Historical Essays on British Columbia* (Toronto: McClelland and Stewart, 1976), pp. 113–21.

47. In his perceptive study of the diplomacy leading to the U.S. acquisition of Alaska, Howard I. Kushner demonstrates the importance of the historical record of American expansion in persuading the czar's government to sell Alaska. See *Conflict on the Northwest Coast: American-Russian Rivalry in the Pacific Northwest, 1790–1867* (Westport, Connecticut: Greenwood Press, 1975).

48. John A. Sutter, Jr., *Statement Regarding Early California Experiences,* ed. Allan R. Ottley (Sacramento: Sacramento Book Collectors Club, 1943), pp. 11–14, 16, 29. Robin W. Winks, *Frederick Billings: A Life* (New York: Oxford University Press, 1991), pp. 40, 45, has new information about Sutter's utterly unbusinesslike behavior after the initial gold rush.

49. John Bidwell to Captain W. F. Swasey, March 12, 1888, in Book Club of California, *Pioneers of the Sacramento,* pp. 26–30.

50. George McKinstry to Lt. Edward M. Kern, San Diego, December 23, 1851, in Dunbar, ed., *Fort Sutter Papers,* MS. 30:1–4.

51. Terry G. Jordan brilliantly analyzes the precedents for American cattle ranching in his book *North American Cattle-Ranching Frontiers* (Albuquerque: University of New Mexico Press, 1993); but see also Thomas D. Clark and John D. W. Guice, *Frontiers in Conflict: The Old Southwest, 1795–1830* (Albuquerque: University of New Mexico Press, 1989), pp. 99–116.

3

John A. Sutter

and the Indian Business

Albert L. Hurtado

John Sutter, as he frequently explained to anyone who might listen, was a man of no small ambitions. Though he arrived in the Sacramento Valley all but destitute, with a tangled record of past financial failure, he expected to accumulate a fortune by building a profitable, flourishing business enterprise in this most remote borderland of Mexican California. Central to Sutter's grand, vastly optimistic plan was his reliance on the native people of the Sacramento region, a fact appreciated by his contemporaries but often ignored by later writers and historical commentators. If we return to a pre-gold-rush appreciation of the importance of the Indian business as a basis for making money in the early West, we will have a truer view of Sutter and the enterprise he called New Helvetia.

In taking up this topic, my intent is to demonstrate the different ways in which Sutter used the Sacramento Valley's Indian resources for his own advantage. Along the way, I hope to clarify Sutter's purpose in coming to this region in the first place, describe some of the models of Indian labor relations that he had observed, and examine the methods that he used to control his Indian labor force. From this inquiry we should gain a fuller appreciation of John Sutter and his times. By focusing on the Indian business, we will be able to define more clearly the historical portrait of Sacramento's pioneer founder, and also gain a fresh perspective concerning the larger human community upon which our own was founded.

Building Blocks of Nascent Capitalism

Sutter did not invent the Indian business. He was a copyist who sought to imitate the success of others who had made fortunes with Indian labor. When Sutter arrived in the United States in 1834, the fur trade was the most obvious of several ways to profit from Indian work. From Hudson's Bay to the Pacific Ocean, large fur companies employed and traded with Indians. Traders happily extended credit to Indian clients who promised to pay up in furs. This arrangement tied Indians and their labor to a commercial economy.[1] Within the United States, it should be added, the federal government cheerfully acted as a bill collector for traders—who were paid when federal agents distributed annual Indian annuities—and the federal government also used Indian indebtedness as a lever to force tribes to cede more land to the young republic.[2] Indian agricultural labor also supported the fur trade; Mandan and Hidatsa farmers peddled food to the traders at the posts on the upper Missouri River.[3]

Indian labor was thus fundamental to the fur trade—a considerable American industry during the early nineteenth century. The wealthy New Yorker John Jacob Astor founded his mighty fortune on the fur trade. Sutter scarcely could have failed to notice that Astor, a fellow immigrant of Germanic origin, was the wealthiest man of his age.[4]

In New Mexico, which like California was part of the Republic of Mexico until 1846, Indian labor was vital to the pastoral economy. Pueblo Indian shepherds tended flocks for missionaries, rancheros, and themselves, wove woolen and cotton fabric for trade with Mexican and Anglo-American merchants who came down the Santa Fé Trail from Missouri. In two centuries of intermittent war, Spaniards, Mexicans, and their Pueblo Indian allies had taken slaves from Apaches, Navajos, and Utes. Some Indian prisoners were sold south to work in the silver mines of Zacatecas, and a few luckless Apaches even reached the auction block in Cuba. Captive children were frequently taken into prosperous New Mexican households, where they worked as servants while learning Spanish and Catholic customs. Numerous enough to form their own community, the progeny of these slaves were known as *genízaros,* which now literally means half-breed but then probably characterized the mixed cultural ancestry of these people. This combination of free and coerced labor reflected labor practices that had provided an economic underpinning for the Spanish Empire from the time of Columbus.[5]

California under Spain and Mexico also relied on Indian labor. The Franciscan missions, which served material as well as religious purposes, were the most important economic institutions in old California. The twenty thousand neophytes who lived and labored in these religious establishments provided the brawn that tended herds, tilled gardens, and made the mission shops hum. When mission properties came into private ownership following Mexican independence, much of the Indian work force as well as mission lands wound up in the hands of rancheros—who were not above attacking native communities in the Central Valley to draft more Indian workmen. Here, too, we find a combination of free labor, slaves, and peons, all laboring among the golden hills of Mexican California in the halcyon days of the hide and tallow trade.[6]

Truly, when Sutter came to America, Indian workers from the Great Lakes to the Pacific and from Mexico to Hudson's Bay were among the building blocks of nascent capitalism. They were not the freeholding farmers that Jefferson revered, nor the merchant capitalists and factory operatives that Hamilton believed would create in the United States a commercial empire to rival Europe. Yet Indian workmen were there in fields, in pastures, in forests, and, yes, even in workshops of the American frontier. Away from America's burgeoning cities and towns, out on the edges of Indian country, in the shaggy fringes of frontier society, native labor was an undeniable part of the scene. Indians took a modest role in some places; in others they were indispensable to the primary purpose of frontier entrepreneurs—to bring western land and resources into the marketplace while reaping profits for themselves. Because this process was distant from eastern cities, new arrivals from Europe might overlook the possibilities of native labor in the continent-wide Indian business; but John A. Sutter had his eyes wide open when he reached the United States, and soon he was in a position to see for himself.

A Tour of Western Enterprise

Although the basic facts of Sutter's American experience before he reached California are well known, a brief summary will emphasize an

important point: Sutter was thoroughly schooled in the Indian business before he arrived in the Sacramento Valley. If he had purposely set out to obtain such an education, he could scarcely have done a better job. After coming to the United States, Sutter did not stay long in New York but headed for Missouri, whose western border faced Indian country and opened to the Santa Fé Trail. Sutter would see much of both.

To mask his business and legal problems in Switzerland, Sutter fabricated an impressive résumé that included a bogus captaincy. With this fictional identity he soon carved out a niche in the German colony near St. Louis. Looking for quicker profits than a settled life could provide, Sutter joined the 1835 Santa Fé caravan. He was not disappointed. Trade was brisk in the Mexican town, and Sutter gained the impression that commercial success was an easy matter. A second Santa Fé trip in 1836 disabused him of naive notions about the profitability of the Southwest. He lost not only his own money but that of other investors as well. Sutter recouped some of his losses by purchasing stolen mustangs from Apaches and selling them to the German burghers who farmed the Missouri bottoms, a transaction that ultimately must have proved less than satisfactory for dude buyers who were unfamiliar with the dangers of working with truly wild horses.

Having worn out a welcome among his countrymen, Sutter moved to Westport, now the site of Kansas City, and traded with the Shawnee and Delaware Indians—a trade which, contrary to U.S. law, included whiskey. By 1838 Sutter was again broke and anxious to leave his debts behind. Determined to put as much distance as possible between himself and his creditors, he decided to go to California, making the first leg of the journey with the American Fur Company's caravan to the Rocky Mountain rendezvous, an annual fur trade fair where mountain men and Indians from all over the region congregated, drank, sported, and did business. On the way to California, he purchased an Indian boy for one hundred dollars, a "large price," according to Sutter.[7] Kit Carson had once owned the boy, who spoke tolerable English and was familiar with some parts of the transcontinental route. It is even possible that the boy was a California native, since Carson had earlier fought Indians and trapped furs within California. Whatever the young man's origins, Sutter took him to the rendezvous; from there he trekked west to Oregon's Willamette Valley, then north to the Hudson's Bay Company Pacific headquarters at Fort Vancouver.

From the Oregon Country, Sutter had intended to head directly south to California, but Hudson's Bay Company men convinced him that he would be foolhardy to attempt such a route with the small party that accompanied him. It would be much safer, he was informed, to sail to Hawaii and then to California. Sutter agreed and, with eight followers who also wanted to go to California, took passage on the "honorable company's" bark *Columbia*. The ship dropped anchor in Honolulu, where he and his party waited for a vessel bound for the mainland.

They waited for several months, but no California-bound ship appeared. In the meantime, as Sutter later claimed, he so impressed the Hawaiian monarch, Kamehameha III, that he received an offer to take command of the island's native army. When Sutter refused, the disappointed king nonetheless provided him with ten indentured servants, two women and "eight men, all experienced seamen—for three years."[8]

Anxious to get to California, Sutter decided to sign on as supercargo of a trading ship bound for the Russian-American Company's headquarters at New Archangel (Sitka), Alaska. The Russian-American Company was a fur outfit specializing in sea otter and seal pelts. Besides the Alaskan operations, as Sutter learned, the Russians also had established Ross Colony in California, an agricultural settlement with its headquarters at Fort Ross, north of Bodega Bay. In Alaska the Russians wined and dined their visitor and revealed more about Sutter's elusive destination.

Finally, Sutter and his small band of followers sailed to California, arriving in San Francisco Bay, then going on to Monterey. Before he embarked for the interior, Sutter visited Fort Ross and stopped at Mariano Vallejo's Sonoma rancho. He also briefly inspected some of the Franciscan mission properties in northern California, where the process of secularization was bringing to an end the missionaries' control over their native converts.

By the time the Swiss entrepreneur and his party paddled up the Sacramento River, Sutter had seen virtually every aspect of the Indian business. He had traded with the Apaches, Shawnees, and Delawares. At Fort Hall, Bent's Fort, Fort Vancouver, and in Alaska, he had seen the fur trade as practiced by Anglo-Americans, Britons, and Russians. He had seen California's missions and ranchos with their Indian labor forces in plain view, and he had witnessed Indian-Hispanic labor relations in Santa Fé. He had seen Indian slaves—he had purchased one—indentured servants, and free workers. A small force of indentured Hawaiians was at his disposal. Surely, in the summer of 1839 there was not a better prepared person to engage in the Indian business in the Sacramento Valley.

Besides accumulating information at the various stops on his grand tour of frontier enterprises, Sutter gathered letters of recommendation from respected westerners.[9] Some of Sutter's biographers have portrayed this exercise as a kind of con game.[10] Certainly, Sutter embellished his reputation, his financial condition, and his business prospects, but the men who endorsed him did not do so because they had been fooled. They recommended him to the attention of their frontier peers precisely because they were *not* fooled. They did not see him as green and untried, a visionary with utopian ideas. They recognized in him a man who appeared as calculating and ruthless as they were. They saw him as a practical man—someone who was quite capable of imitating their own accomplishments. And that is precisely what Sutter did.

The Central Valley Indian Resource

In 1839 perhaps forty to fifty thousand Indians lived in the Sacramento Valley, with a like number in the San Joaquin.[11] Before the arrival of Europeans, the people of Central California hunted, fished, and gathered wild foods. They did not practice agriculture because they had no need for it. The temperate climate and a variety of food resources made for an abundant and relatively easy life without tilling the fertile valley land. This is not to say that California Indians were lazy or somehow backward. They took each plant and game animal in its season, following a fairly constant round of activity from spring through fall, and during the winter they devoted much time to the cycle of religious ceremonies and dancing now known as the Kuksu cult. To live through the lean winter, of course, Indians had to amass surplus food during the warm seasons—a fact that argues well for their industriousness. The absence of agriculture did not reflect a lack of Indian ambition or aptitude, but demonstrated how well they practiced the life of hunting and gathering.[12]

Indians divided labor according to gender. Women's work revolved around the harvest and preparation of grass seeds, berries, tubers, and the ubiquitous acorn. This latter food the women ground into flour with a stone muller or with a pestle in a bowl or a bedrock mortar. Then they placed the flour in a sandy depression near a stream and poured water through it to leach out the bitter tannin. The women cooked the flour as a kind of nutritious mush and prepared other foods from it as well. They also cooked the fish and meat that the men brought back. Besides culinary duties, women also made baskets and other utensils from grasses and willow bark. California Indians still are noted basket weavers; the traditional basketry skull cap symbolized women's work and the weaver's skill throughout the region.

Men's work included hunting deer, elk, and antelope that grazed on the valley's vast grasslands. Before the advent of metal goods, men chipped stone projectile points for their hunting arrows and lances. Likewise, they made stone knives and scrapers with which to butcher meat and dress skins. Indians fished with spears, traps, and nets. To improve their efficiency, Indian fishermen built substantial weirs (or fish dams) to concentrate their prey. Central California natives also relied on small game, rodents, and insects as sources of protein, often using fire as an aid to their hunting and gathering.[13]

The traditional skills of California Indians did not immediately become obsolete when Europeans appeared. Native technology and knowledge of local ecology were important resources on a raw, isolated frontier, and Europeans were prepared to take full advantage of them until other resources were available. Long before Sutter came, however, Indians had added new skills to their credentials as workers. At the end of the eighteenth century, Franciscan missionaries began to recruit neophytes in the California interior. Until the Mexican civil government issued secularization orders in 1834, thousands of Plains Miwok and Valley Yokuts went to the missions in the coastal region. Missions were supposed to teach Indians European trades as well as the Catholic faith. Accordingly, former interior Indians learned to plant and harvest crops, ride horses, tend cattle, weave textiles, make adobe blocks, and build the structures that were the architectural hallmark of the California missions.[14]

Many Miwok and Yokuts neophytes became disenchanted with the missions and returned to the valley. Often they took livestock from mission herds; horses were their favorite target. In training a labor force, Hispanic Californians had thus taught Indians a body of skills that made them formidable enemies and very efficient horse thieves. Established on the tributaries of the San Joaquin River, the so-called horse-thief Indians were the bane of Spanish, Mexican, and early Anglo-American California. The Miwok who lived between the Cosumnes and Stanislaus rivers were the most vigorous of these raiders, and the Muquelemne Miwok were the most feared.

In 1827 Jedediah Smith opened California to the Anglo-American fur trade and introduced interior Indians to mountain men and their ways. Beaver pelts were the primary object of Smith and those who followed in his wake, but they also noticed another valuable California resource, horses and mules. Some traders, like Smith, purchased horses from Mexican owners and sold them at the rendezvous and points as far east as Missouri. Other, less scrupulous traders—Jedediah Smith reputedly carried a Bible, did not swear, and lived an otherwise upstanding Christian life—did not bother to secure legal title to California horses. Instead they traded with the Miwok and Yokuts raiders who rustled from Mexican herds. In the 1830s and 1840s, Anglo-American traders and their Indian accomplices made off with thousands of California horses, destined for markets east of the Rocky Mountains. Thus California blood stock contributed to the ancestry of the famed Missouri mule.

Though it was illicit from the Mexican perspective, rustling was a part of the California Indian business. The Indians who worked at this dangerous trade had skills that should not be underestimated. To steal a herd of horses and ride fast and hard over long distances through broken terrain at night, while eluding pursuing California vaqueros (according to some admirers, the finest light horsemen in the world), was not an easy trick. Hispanic Californians were unable to put a stop to this long-distance rustling, and Anglo-American authorities did no better until the gold rush shifted the demographic balance of the Indian and white populations.[15]

From Sutter's perspective, the interior Indians were a labor resource with a variety of traditional and new skills that enhanced their value as workers. Some among these people offered the prospect of a basic native labor pool already familiar with agriculture and livestock herding. But as Sutter would soon learn, these native Californians could prove to be a challenging as well as a useful labor force. They had already gained plenty of experience with white men, and they had their own ideas about the utility of Sutter's New Helvetia project.

Musket, Lash, and Gibbet

Sutter had no illusions about finding docile Indians in the Sacramento Valley. He intended to establish friendly relations with them, but realized that force might be needed to maintain his small force of intruders. Though the Nisenan Indians were initially friendly, the lord of New Helvetia came equipped with brass cannons that his men mounted and prepared for firing when they made camp on the American River. Upon the departure of the vessels that had carried him up the Sacramento, Sutter had his cannoneers fire a nine-gun salute that made a lasting impression on William Heath Davis:

> A large number of deer, elk and other animals on the plains were startled, running to and fro, stopping to listen, their heads raised, full of curiosity and wonder, seemingly attracted and fascinated to the spot, while from the interior of the adjacent wood the howls of wolves and coyotes filled the air, and immense flocks of waterfowl flew wildly over the camp.[16]

Sutter remembered firing his cannons, too, but not merely to salute the departing boats. "To show the Indians the effect of powder & ball," Sutter recalled, "I planted my guns and fired at a target. They did not care to have them tried on them."[17] Sutter, it should go without saying, had not brought cannons to the Sacramento Valley to hunt deer, but to overpower Indians who resisted his authority.

Sutter was either lucky or wise in his selection of the site for New Helvetia. He settled in Nisenan country near the villages of Pusune and Momol, just north of Miwok territory. Occupying a borderland between the Miwok and the Nisenan, Sutter was able to play off these groups against each other.[18]

The Nisenan had been in contact with Anglo-American and British fur traders, and had suffered greatly from a malaria epidemic that swept the valley in 1833.[19] Unlike the Miwok, Nisenan people had not entered the Spanish missions, though some former mission Indians had evidently settled among them.

Despite a few early attempts to oust Sutter, most of the Nisenan quickly accommodated, joined his work force, and helped him to assert his influence among interior Indians. The Miwok, on the other hand, remained largely antagonistic to Sutter and preferred to maintain their independence in the San Joaquin Valley. Indians who accepted Sutter responded not only to force, but also to the advantages that Sutter's presence offered: a steady supply of trade goods and protection from Indian and Mexican enemies. Moreover, new diseases like malaria, smallpox, and measles had ravaged the Indian population, leaving them in a debilitated condition and less able to resist. Indian responses to Sutter were divided more or less along tribal lines, but it must be admitted that some Nisenan never accepted Sutter and some Miwok readily joined the coterie of Indians, Mexicans, British and Anglo-American fur traders, and Hawaiians who founded Sacramento's modern multiethnic society.

Sutter, of course, was not a social experimenter bent on creating a new community based on racial equality, but a hardheaded realist determined to put the valley's human capital to work. Wage labor was an important part of Sutter's master plan; whenever he could, he paid Indians for their labor. He did not do so, however, merely because he believed in an honest day's pay for an honest day's labor, but because the payment of wages and the extension of credit provided Sutter with more control over Indian workers. His system was simple and effective. He issued metal disks to Indian workers, who wore them as pendants on necklaces. After they had worked for a standard period of time, Sutter punched a distinctive hole in the disk. Each hole represented a monetary value that Indians could redeem only at Sutter's store. Heinrich Lienhard, one of Sutter's white overseers, recalled that Indians had to work about two weeks to receive enough credit to purchase a pair of cotton trousers or a plain muslin shirt. Other trade goods—metalware, blankets, weapons—were no doubt priced accordingly.[20] Like other Indian traders, Sutter extended credit to his customers and secured a lien on Indian labor in the future. Thus Sutter created a primitive form of currency and a system of debt and credit with which he controlled wages and prices in New Helvetia.

Because we are all now caught in the web of money, debt, and credit, some may ask whether that was such a bad thing for Indians. For some individual Indians such a system might have worked well because it provided a fairly reliable livelihood. However, labor in New Helvetia drew adult male Indians away from rancherías, leaving the women, children, and elderly unprotected. The Indian working days symbolized in Sutter's tin currency were not available for traditional Indian pursuits. Blankets, clothing, and beads could not replace traditional foods, which went unharvested at the proper times. However attractive the short-term rewards, wage labor in the long run thus tended to break down Indian community life while undercutting the customary native economy.

And what did Indian workers do for Sutter at New Helvetia? The short answer is that they did virtually everything. They caught fish, and salted and packed them in barrels for shipment to South America. They trapped beaver and otters and cured the pelts for the fur trade. They killed deer and elk, rendered tallow, and stored salted meat in barrels. They tanned hides, made leather goods, produced felt, blocked hats, wove blankets, and distilled brandy. Indians made the mud and shaped the bricks and then laid them in courses to form the walls of Sutter's Fort. They dug ditches, plowed furrows, and sowed, weeded, reaped, thrashed, winnowed, and gleaned Sutter's wheat. Indian hands bagged, stored, and ground grain to flour, and then baked it into bread. Indian vaqueros herded, branded, killed, and butchered New Helvetia cattle.[21]

Sutter provided a frank description of the magnitude and variety of his Indian work force:

> Business increased until I had in the harvest 600 men, & to feed them I had to kill four oxen, sometimes five daily. . . . I had at the same time twelve thousand head of cattle and two thousand horses, and ten or fifteen thousand sheep. I had all the Indians I could employ. There were thirty plows with fresh oxen running every morning. I had looms and taught the natives to weave blankets and [to make] hats. My best days were just before the gold discovery.[22]

When Sutter reminisced about the flush days of early California, he thought of a time when he had all the Indians he could employ. Even in old age Sutter still appreciated the simple calculus of the Indian business. Cheap Indian labor plus abundant natural resources made profits. Sutter hired white skilled labor and overseers whenever he could, and historians have emphasized the presence of the few white craftsmen who worked at the fort.[23] But it was the labor of the Indian majority that created a demand for the services of the white minority. What, we might ask, would a cooper do at Sutter's Fort without the agricultural production of those hundreds of Indian hands? And we can also imagine that Indians helped white craftsmen, cleaned the shops, stoked the blacksmith's fires, drew the water, cut the wood, and attended to the dozens of errands that arose in the course of any crafts-man's work day.

Sutter's great success at New Helvetia was in managing the local Indian population for his own purposes. In this he replicated the achievements of Anglo-American, British, and Russian traders and trappers, Franciscan missionaries, California rancheros, and sundry others who relied on Indian labor in the Far West. Indian labor was at the very center of Captain Sutter's vision for a vast and thriving New Helvetia, and his fortunes rose and fell with his ability to command native workers.

Nobody, of course, understood this better than Sutter. His corre-spondence is full of references to his Indian labor needs. Determined to secure that labor, he was willing to use any means at his disposal to get it.[24] The fort was emblematic of Sutter's ambition and authority then, and it remains so today. But the fort was not merely a symbol, for it housed an Indian army of perhaps two hundred men supervised by white officers. After Sutter purchased Fort Ross, he dressed his army in Russian uniforms of blue and green.[25] An outlandish image, is it not? Yet it was part of the daily routine at Sutter's Fort.

This Indian army was a vital part of Sutter's Indian business and a force to be reckoned with in Mexican California. It enabled him to protect his fort, fields, and herds against Miwok raiders. He marched his army against the troublesome Muquelemne Miwok to the south and recounted these exploits with pride.[26] When disaffected *Califor-nios* rebelled against the Mexican government, Governor Manuel Mi-cheltorena called Sutter and his army to service in southern California. Though the army was not defeated, Sutter managed to blunder into enemy hands, and his force surrendered.[27] Nevertheless, the victo-rious *Californios* permitted Sutter and his Indian troops to return to the Sacramento Valley, where they protected Mexican herds in the coastal valleys against the forays of Miwok horse raiders. During the Mexican War these Indians enlisted in the American army and helped to secure California for the United States. Thus Nisenan and Miwok soldiers became unheralded veterans of a war between foreigners in their native land.[28]

The primary purpose of this Indian force, however, was to control Indians in the Sacramento and San Joaquin valleys. As Sutter explained to his overseer, Pierson B. Reading, if the Indians were "not kept strickly under fear, it will be no good."[29] Indian communities that violated New Helvetia's unwritten laws risked armed attack, and individual Indians faced corporal punishment from Sutter. Nevertheless, Indians defied Sutter's authority, fled from his service, and instigated rebellions.

Rufino and Raphero, two Miwok men, became central figures in the most dramatic example of Sutter's use of violence to control the Indians at Sutter's Fort. Rufino worked for Sutter while his kinsman Raphero followed the life of a horse raider with the Muquelemne Miwok. Sutter captured Raphero, executed him, and affixed his head over the gate of Sutter's Fort, where one of Sutter's employees saw "the long black hair and skull. . . ."[30] Sutter no doubt intended this grisly trophy to deter Indian rebellion; it remained on display for some time. Sutter misjudged the impact of his actions, however, for the execution of Raphero outraged Rufino. In apparent retaliation, Rufino killed his own brother-in-law, a loyal member of Sutter's army, and fled from New Helvetia. For months Sutter hunted for Rufino, who was finally captured and killed in September 1845. But the lord of New Helvetia did not put Rufino's head on display next to Raphero's.[31] Evidently Sutter decided not to push his luck again.

Sutter recorded Rufino's execution in his New Helvetia Diary with a single terse sentence that mixed punishment and business with hardly a pause: "Rufino chief of the Moquelumnes, was tried for murder, found guilty, and executed—started D. Martin for lumber."[32] Life went on at New Helvetia. The execution of an Indian was just a part of daily affairs at the fort, a matter of fact and barely remarkable. We do not even know if Sutter built a gallows and hanged Rufino, or put him up against one of the fort's walls before an Indian firing squad. Perhaps the killing was perfunctory, unaccompanied by the grim pomp and ceremony of public execution one hundred forty-five years ago, and now just a footnote to Sutter's Indian business.

The Trade in Indian Persons

One more aspect of Sutter's Indian business must be given attention, and that is Indian slavery. While it is true that Sutter paid his Indian workers most of the time, he also used his Indian army to capture native people who were reluctant to work voluntarily. Sometimes he held these dragooned workers in stock pens; when there was space he locked them in rooms at the fort to keep them from escaping at night.[33] Indian labor was in greatest demand at harvest time. Without machinery, Sutter was utterly dependent on stoop labor to get in his wheat and other crops, and he was always at pains to find enough workmen during the long harvest season.

John Bidwell, another of Sutter's employees, has left us a compelling description of Indians at this backbreaking work.

> Imagine three or four hundred wild Indians in a grain field armed, some with sickles, some with butcher-knives, some with pieces of hoop iron roughly fashioned into shapes like sickles, but others having only their hands with which to gather up by small handfuls the dry and brittle grain; and as their hands would become sore, they resorted to dry willow sticks, which were split to sever the straw.[34]

No wonder that some Indians were unwilling to volunteer for this work. No wonder that Sutter used his army to drive shanghaied workers into the fields.

But Sutter's use of Indian slaves did not stop there. He also found profit in selling and leasing Indians to other landholders. Little documentary record remains of these transactions, although evidence suggests that at one point Sutter derived about one-third of his income from leasing Indians to others.[35] Ordinarily Sutter fed his Indian workers, and he insisted that those who leased his labor force do likewise. But when times were hard, Sutter could neither feed nor clothe Indian laborers. John Marsh complained in 1845 that one gang of these leased workmen arrived at his place "as usual, dying of hunger."[36]

Records of the outright sale of Indians are sketchy. John Chamberlain, Sutter's blacksmith, reported that it was "customary for Capt Sutter to buy and sell Indian boys and girls at New Helvetia."[37] Sutter's correspondence suggests some unsavory aspects of this trade. He promised to send one Mexican ranchero thirty young Indians after a "campaign against the horse-thieves."[38] We may assume that these captives were not free agents competing in an open marketplace. Some of Sutter's clients requested young girls, and Sutter complied, although he evidently had some misgivings. In sending two girls to William Leidesdorff he wrote that Leidesdorff should take the one "which you like the best, the *other* is for Mr. Ridley, whom I promised one longer as two year's ago." And then he continued, "As this shall never be considered an article of trade [I] make you a present with this girl."[39] Sutter's logic is difficult to comprehend in this matter. When he turned the young girls into gifts for his male friends, they did indeed become "articles of trade." One does not make a gift of a free human being.

It is tempting to compare New Helvetia Indian labor to the slave-based plantation economy in the antebellum South, but the comparison does not quite work. Certainly there were similarities: slavery, the lash, a trade in Indian persons. But New Helvetia did not depend primarily on a slave labor system. Probably the majority, perhaps a large majority, of Indian workers were free. No doubt some of these workers opted for wage labor because of the ever-present threat of force, but some (we will never know how many) freely chose to work for Sutter because it seemed to be advantageous. Wage labor gave Indians access to new material goods at Sutter's store. And, after all, Indians who entered the labor force were by no means unique. People the world over have been abandoning barter and subsistence economies for hundreds of years. I will stop short of saying that it is human nature to do so, but this movement into a commercial, money-based economy is one of the major themes of human history. Indians who worked for Sutter showed that they were flexible and that they shared some of the traits of other people in other times who have made similar choices.[40]

Although individual Indians may have benefited from wage labor, overall the New Helvetia economy had a negative influence on the Indian population. Census records show that Sutter employed far more men than women; hence women, children, and old people were left unprotected when men were at work. Slave raiders from the coast found these defenseless villages tempting targets, though Sutter tried to restrain such invasions.[41]

In addition, Indians who worked for Sutter risked infection with many newly introduced diseases. Because of their centuries of biological isolation from Europe, Asia, and Africa, America's native peoples lacked any genetic resistance or acquired immunities to a wide range of illnesses unknown in the western hemisphere before the Euro-American invasion. As a result, smallpox, measles, influenza, and other communicable epidemic diseases killed Indians in immense numbers throughout the hemisphere. Locally, in addition to the earlier introduction of malaria, the consequences of this disease frontier were dramatically revealed when a measles epidemic swept the valley in the summer of 1847. Sutter recorded the disease's progress, along with his repeated attempts to recruit replacements for his sick and dying labor force. To his credit, Sutter employed a physician to cure sick Indians, but of course mid-nineteenth-century medicine was totally ineffective against this and similar outbreaks.[42] Thus, employment with Sutter imposed also a mortal tax on the Indian population, a tax that fell due with dreadful regularity.

The gold rush rapidly changed the California economy. Sutter's primitive monetary monopoly quickly ended as gold dust, coin, and regular currency came into circulation. At first he tried to benefit by contracting Indian labor to early mine operators.[43] But, as more and more white newcomers entered the Mother Lode region and insisted—often by force of arms—that they would not tolerate the competition of any nonwhite, servile work force in the placer diggings, Indian labor quickly fell out of favor. Finally Sutter retired to Hock Farm on the Feather River, where he continued to rely on Indian labor. Much to his surprise, however, the conditions of employment for Indian farm workers were also changing. Native workers demanded cash, while Sutter preferred to give them old clothes, just as he had done at Sutter's Fort. Consequently, Sutter was unable to secure their services—at least not on the terms that he remembered so fondly from his best years in New Helvetia.

In 1856 Sutter was nearly broke and about to lose his farm. With creditors pressing from every side, he made a last-ditch attempt to resurrect the labor patterns of the past. He wrote to the superintendent of Indian affairs for California, Thomas Henley, the official responsible for carrying out federal Indian policy in the Golden State. The Indians near his farm, Sutter claimed, were out of control. They refused to work for less than a dollar a day and, in Sutter's opinion, spent their money unwisely on liquor in Marysville. Many of them preferred to work for wages in the town rather than in Sutter's fields. As Sutter put it in his characteristic broken English, "nothing as the Dollars could bring them to work." The Nisenan, who had formerly worked willingly for the lord of New Helvetia, "dont like more to work unless they are paid more as they earn."[44]

A little translation is in order here. Sutter was upset because Indians demanded an honest day's wages for a long day's work. They wanted to be free to work for whomever they pleased, and to spend their cash on whatever they wanted. This simply would not do for Sutter's purposes, and he had a remedy in mind. He advised the superintendent to take the most troublesome Nisenan to a reservation, and "give me the Control *only of the* Hock and Yukulme Indians, I would make them work and pay them a reasonable compensation in food and Clothing. And when they know that it is your Order, they will do so, in preference of leaving the Grounds where they are born and where their Ancestors have dwelled."[45]

Though this request contravened federal Indian policy, the superintendent acceded to Sutter's wishes because, as Henley recorded, he was "the Pioneer of California; and his character for hospitality, generosity, and true friendship for the Indians is proverbial."[46] In 1856 Sutter's credentials in the Indian business were impeccable with federal officials, if not with Indians. However, this arrangement did not save Sutter, since his debtors foreclosed on the Hock Farm property in 1857. Somehow he managed to redeem his property, and he remained in California until 1865, when an arsonist burned him out. Poverty-stricken and dispirited, and relying on a pension from the state government, he then left California for good.[47] By then, Sutter had been in the Indian business for about thirty years.

During those decades Sutter was renowned for his hospitality to immigrants, and he was also respected for his ability to work with Indians. Whites regarded him as a model: just as he at first copied the techniques of the leading frontier entrepreneurs of his age, newcomers had imitated Sutter. John Bidwell, Pierson Reading, and many other of

Sutter's white employees acquired ranchos and Indian workers much as he had done. Charles Weber and Thomas Savage opened the southern mines and employed Indians in mines and on ranchos.[48] Even the federal government noticed Sutter's success and appointed him Indian agent during the Mexican War, a position that he resigned due to the press of business affairs after gold was discovered.[49]

The first federal reservations in California were meant to be self-sufficient using Indian labor, an idea inspired in part by the missions and partly by Sutter's operations at New Helvetia.[50] So Sutter's fame and influence as the leading California pioneer were based largely on his success in the Indian business—which was the main business of New Helvetia.

A few figures help to underscore that basic point. In 1847 about 280 white men, women, and children were associated in one way or another with New Helvetia. At the same time the New Helvetia area was home to about 2,800 Indian men, women, and children.[51] Some were workers, some were soldiers, and there were many women and children carrying on traditional pursuits in their rancherías. In effect, even nonworkers subsidized New Helvetia by providing a population from which workers could be drawn, and by providing subsistence for workers when they were not employed. The native villages, in other words, offered to Sutter a rudimentary system of unemployment compensation, medical care, and disability and retirement support—all at no cost. One way or another, Indians were New Helvetia. None of its work, none of Sutter's accomplishments, would have been possible without the Indian majority who furnished labor, food, and even a market for Sutter's trade goods.

Of Saints Secular and Religious

So what are we to make of all this? Certainly Sutter's career in the Indian business was unsavory. He ruthlessly exploited Indians however he could, giving no thought to the consequences for them. While his enterprises provided incomes, power, and status for some Indians, Sutter directly contributed to the weakening of Indian autonomy and the decline of Indian numbers in the Sacramento Valley. To view him as a benefactor of Indians—as Henley did in 1856, and as some historical commentators do even now—simply ignores evidence that is plain and abundant.

Richard Dillon's recently reissued biography of Sutter speaks of him as Sacramento's sainted sinner. Indeed, Sutter the pioneer hero has become a sort of secular saint, and as such begs comparison with California's Roman Catholic saint-in-waiting, Junípero Serra. Though widely separated in time and motivated by very different impulses, both Serra and Sutter reside in the pantheon of California's pioneer heroes. Grade-school children learn of each of these men as they march through the glorious procession of Golden State history. Serra came first, a godly man who wanted to bring Christianity to the Indians. The colorful and photogenic missions that remain along Highway 101 today are the architectural legacy of his evangelical career. Then came Sutter, friend to white immigrants and Indians alike. Well-meaning public officials name schools for these men and others like them. Well-meaning teachers and historical museum curators teach young people about their great deeds, perpetuating old myths. It is comfortable to remember a beatific Serra and a kindly Sutter, surrounded by friendly Indians. It is easy to overlook the whipping post and, in Sutter's case, the execution wall.

We should not wonder that some people are surprised when critics challenge the mythic past, as happened during the recent controversy over Father Serra. While many Californians were waiting to celebrate the final canonization of the Franciscan pioneer, Indians spoiled the party by reminding everyone that the missions ushered in a period of population decline and that Serra—like Sutter—resorted to corporal punishment.[52] It should come as no shock to learn that many California Indians would prefer to have the State Indian Museum relocated someplace away from its present site in the fort's backyard.

For Indians, the fort is a symbol of something quite different than the image portrayed in grade-school textbooks. They know that Sutter's Fort is about the Indian business. Without Indians, there would have been no fort, no New Helvetia; it is hard to imagine how Sutter could then have become known as one of California's premier pioneers. Whatever Sutter's successes and failures, Indians paid the price.

Notes

1. The fur trade literature is huge. For interpretive treatments of the impact of the trade on Indians, see David J. Wishart, *The Fur Trade and the American*

West, 1807–1840 (Lincoln: University of Nebraska Press, 1979); Calvin Martin, *Keepers of the Game: Indian-Animal Relationships and the Fur Trade* (Berkeley: University of California Press, 1978); William Cronon, *Changes in the Land: Indians, Colonists, and the Ecology of New England* (New York: Hill and Wang, 1983); James P. Ronda, *Lewis and Clark among the Indians* (Lincoln: University of Nebraska Press, 1984); and Richard White, *The Roots of Dependency: Subsistence, Environment, and Social Change among the Choctaws, Pawnees, and Navajos* (Lincoln: University of Nebraska Press, 1983). On the Canadian trade, see Arthur J. Ray, *Indians in the Fur Trade: Their Role as Hunters, Trappers, and Middlemen in the Lands Southwest of Hudson Bay, 1660–1870* (Toronto: University of Toronto Press, 1974); Arthur J. Ray and Donald Freeman, *"Give Us Good Measure": An Economic Analysis of Relations between the Indians and the Hudson's Bay Company before 1763* (Toronto: University of Toronto Press, 1978); and W. J. Eccles, "The Fur Trade and Eighteenth-Century Imperialism," *William and Mary Quarterly* 40 (1983): 341–62.

2. White, *Roots of Dependency,* pp. 95–96; and Robert A. Trennert, Jr., *Indian Traders on the Middle Border: The House of Ewing, 1827–54* (Lincoln: University of Nebraska Press, 1981), pp. 114–16 *et passim.*

3. James A. Bennyhoff, *Ethnogeography of the Plains Miwok,* Center for Archaeological Research at Davis, no. 5 (Davis: University of California, 1977).

4. James P. Ronda, *Astoria and Empire* (Lincoln: University of Nebraska Press, 1990).

5. Robert Archibald, "Acculturation and Assimilation in Colonial New Mexico," *New Mexico Historical Quarterly* 53 (1978): 205–17; and Christon I. Archer, "The Deportation of the Barbarian Indians from the Internal Provinces of New Spain," *Americas* 29 (1973): 376–85. On the Columbian origins of Spanish labor practices, see Carl Ortwin Sauer, *The Early Spanish Main* (Berkeley: University of California Press, 1969), pp. 66–67; and Charles Gibson, *Spain in America* (New York: Harper and Row, 1966), pp. 48–67.

6. Sherburne F. Cook, *The Indian versus the Spanish Mission,* Ibero-Americana 21 (Berkeley: University of California Press, 1943); Sherburne F. Cook, *The Physical and Demographic Reaction of Nonmission Indians in Colonial and Provincial California,* Ibero-Americana 22 (Berkeley: University of California Press, 1943); Robert Archibald, "The Economy of the Alta California Mission, 1803–1821," *Southern California Quarterly* 58 (1976): 227–40; and Albert L. Hurtado, "California Indians and the Workaday West: Labor, Assimilation, and Survival," *California History* 69 (1990): 2–11.

7. John Augustus Sutter, "Personal Reminiscences of General John Augustus Sutter," MS, Bancroft Library, University of California, Berkeley (hereafter cited as Sutter, "Reminiscences").

8. Sutter, "Reminiscences."

9. Richard Dillon, *Fool's Gold: The Decline and Fall of Captain John Sutter of California* (New York: Coward-McCann, 1967; reprint, Santa Cruz, California: Western Tanager, 1981), p. 75; and Erwin G. Gudde, *Sutter's Own Story: The Life of General John Augustus Sutter and the History of New Helvetia in the Sacramento Valley* (New York: G. P. Putnam's Sons, 1936), p. 25.

10. See, for example, James Peter Zollinger, *Sutter: The Man and His Empire* (New York: Oxford University Press, 1939), pp. 44–45; and Marguerite Eyer Wilbur's fictionalized biography, *John Sutter: Rascal and Adventurer* (New York: Liveright Publishing Corporation, 1949), 42–46.

11. Sherburne F. Cook, *The Population of the California Indians, 1769–1970* (Berkeley: University of California Press, 1976), p. 42. Cook gives the figures as 76,100 and 83,800 respectively, but this estimate was for the period prior to the introduction of European diseases that devastated the populations. The numbers that I give in the text are extrapolated from Cook's calculations.

12. Robert F. Heizer and Albert B. Elsasser, *The Natural World of the California Indians* (Berkeley: University of California Press, 1980), pp. 37–45.

13. Lowell John Bean, "Social Organization in Native California," in *Native Californians: A Theoretical Retrospective,* ed. Lowell John Bean and Thomas C. Blackburn (Socorro, New Mexico: Ballena Press, 1976), pp. 99–124; Joseph L. Chartkoff and Kerry Kona Chartkoff, *The Archeology of California* (Stanford: Stanford University Press, 1984), pp. 205–42; and Robert F. Heizer, ed., *Handbook of North American Indians,* vol. 8, *California* (Washington, D.C.: Smithsonian Institution, 1978), pp. 370–97.

14. Albert L. Hurtado, *Indian Survival on the California Frontier* (New Haven: Yale University Press, 1988), pp. 24, 32–35; and Edith Buckland Webb, *Indian Life at the Old Missions* (Los Angeles: W. F. Lewis Publications, 1952; reprint, Lincoln: University of Nebraska Press, 1982).

15. Hurtado, *Indian Survival,* pp. 32–54.

16. William Heath Davis, *Seventy-five Years in California: Recollections and Remarks by One Who Visited These Shores in 1831, and again in 1833, and Except When Absent on Business Was a Resident from 1838 until the End of a Long Life in 1909,* ed. Harold A. Small, 3d ed. (San Francisco: J. Howell Books, 1967), p. 16.

17. Sutter, "Reminiscences."

18. Bennyhoff, *Ethnogeography of the Plains Miwok.*

19. Sherburne F. Cook, *The Epidemic of 1830–1833 in California and Oregon,* University of California Publications in American Archaeology and Ethnology 43 , no. 3 (1955): 303–25.

20. Sutter, "Reminiscences"; and Heinrich Lienhard, *A Pioneer at Sutter's Fort, 1846–1850: The Adventures of Heinrich Lienhard,* trans. and ed. Marguerite Eyer Wilbur (Los Angeles: Calafía Society, 1941), p. 68.

21. Sutter, "Reminiscences"; Webfoot [William D. Phelps], *Fore and Aft; Or, Leaves from the Life of an Old Sailor* (Boston: Nichols and Hall, 1871), p. 258; Sutter to William A. Leidesdorff, August 8, 1844, MS. 22, Leidesdorff Collection, Henry E. Huntington Library, San Marino, California (hereafter cited as LC); and Sutter to Antonio Suñol, May 14 and June 13, 1842, Sutter Collection, California Room, State Library, Sacramento, California (hereafter cited as SuC).

22. Sutter, "Reminiscences."

23. Dillon, *Fool's Gold,* pp. 206–8, 221–22, emphasizes Sutter's self-interest in encouraging immigrants to settle near him.

24. See for examples Sutter to Pierson B. Reading, May 11, 1845, Reading Collection, California Room, State Library, Sacramento, California (hereafter cited as RC); John A. Sutter et al., *New Helvetia Diary: A Record of Events Kept by John A. Sutter and His Clerks at New Helvetia, California, from September 9, 1845, to May 25, 1848* (San Francisco: Grabhorn Press, 1939), pp. 50–96; and Sutter to William A. Leidesdorff, April 17, 1846, MS. 122, and May 11, 1846, MS. 129, LC.

25. Sutter, "Reminiscences."

26. Sutter, "Reminiscences"; and Johann August Sutter, *The Diary of Johann August Sutter* (San Francisco: Grabhorn Press, 1932), p. 8.

27. Sutter, "Reminiscences."

28. Sutter, "Reminiscences"; John S. Missroon to Edward Kern, August 8, 1846, MS. 27, and August 16, 1846, MS. 28, Fort Sutter Papers, Henry E. Huntington Library (hereafter cited as FSP); John B. Montgomery to Edward Kern, August 26, 1846, MS. 63, FSP; Edwin Bryant, *What I Saw in California: Being the Journal of a Tour by the Emigrant Route and South Pass of the Rocky Mountains, across the Continent of North America, the Great Desert Basin, and*

through California in the Years 1846, 1847 (New York: D. Appleton and Company, 1848; reprint, Berkeley: University of California Press, 1985), pp. 359–60; "Muster Roll of Company H," February 18, 1847, Selected Records of the General Accounting Office Relating to the Frémont Expeditions and the California Battalion, 1842–1890, Records of the United States General Accounting Office, Record Group 217, National Archives Microfilm Publication T135; and Donald Jackson and Mary Lee Spence, eds., *The Expeditions of John Charles Frémont,* 3 vols. (Urbana: University of Illinois Press, 1970–73), 2:235 and 302.

29. Sutter to Pierson B. Reading, May 8, 1845, RC.

30. Heinrich Lienhard described Raphero's head in *Pioneer at Sutter's Fort,* p. 3.

31. Sutter to Pierson B. Reading, February 15, 1845, RC; and Sutter et al., *New Helvetia Diary,* p. 2.

32. Sutter et al., *New Helvetia Diary,* p. 2.

33. The account about stock pens was attributed to Lizzie Enos, a prominent Maidu woman, by Bernice Pate of Auburn, California, in an interview with author, July 1, 1976. For other stories by and about Lizzie Enos, see Richard Simpson, *Ooti: A Maidu Legacy* (Milbrae, California: Celestial Arts, 1977). On housing within the fort, see Lienhard, *Pioneer at Sutter's Fort,* p. 68. On using force to control Indian workers, see Sutter to Antonio Suñol, May 19, 1845, SuC; Sutter to Pierson B. Reading, May 11, 1845, RC.

34. John Bidwell, *Echoes of the Past about California,* and John Steele, *In Camp and Cabin,* 2 vols. in 1, ed. Milo Milton Quaife (Chicago: R. R. Donnelly and Sons, 1928), pp. 82–83.

35. Account of W. A. Leidesdorff, August 1, 1844, to January 27, 1846, MS. 32, Marsh Collection, California Room, State Library, Sacramento (hereafter cited as MC).

36. John Marsh to Antonio Suñol, March 16, 1845, MC.

37. John Chamberlain, "Memoirs of California since 1840," MS, Bancroft Library, University of California, Berkeley.

38. Sutter to Antonio Suñol, May 19, 1845, SuC.

39. Sutter to William A. Leidesdorff, May 11, 1846, MS. 129, LC.

40. See the discussion in Fernand Braudel, *Civilization and Capitalism, 15th–18th Century,* vol. 1, *The Structures of Everyday Life,* trans. Siân Reynolds (New York: Harper & Row, 1981), pp. 93–102 *et passim.* At the same time, we should

recognize that Sutter's reliance on Indian enslavement provided him with a margin of available cheap labor at a time when labor was scarce. Indian slavery may well have made for John Sutter the critical difference between profit and loss during New Helvetia's most prosperous years; see Hurtado, *Indian Survival*, pp. 59–60. On forced labor as an alternative to free labor in regions of frontier commercial and agricultural expansion, see Howard R. Lamar, "From Bondage to Contract: Ethnic Labor in the American West, 1600–1890," in *The Countryside in the Age of Capitalist Transformation: Essays in the Social History of Rural America*, ed. Steven Hahn and Jonathan Prud (Chapel Hill: University of North Carolina Press, 1985); Peter Kolchin, *Unfree Labor: American Slavery and Russian Serfdom* (Cambridge, Massachusetts: Harvard University Press, 1987); and Thomas Barfield, *The Perilous Frontier: Nomadic Empires and China* (Cambridge: Basil Blackwell, 1989).

41. Census data are in [George McKinstry], November 1846, MSS. 12–13, McKinstry Papers, Bancroft Library, University of California, Berkeley (hereafter cited as MKP); and Sutter, "Estimate of Indian Population," December 20, 1847, MSS. 14–15, MKP. The best known slave-raiding episode is described in Sutter to José de Jesus Vallejo, October 15, 1840, SuC.

42. Sutter et al., *New Helvetia Diary*, pp. 58–101; and Robert F. Heizer, "Walla Walla Indian Expeditions to the Sacramento Valley," *California Historical Society Quarterly* 21 (1942): 1–7.

43. Sutter, *Diary*, pp. 45–46.

44. Sutter to Thomas Henley, February 9, 1856, Letters Received by the Office of Indian Affairs, California Superintendency, 1849–1880, Records of the Bureau of Indian Affairs, Record Group 75, National Archives Microfilm Publication M234, reel 35 (hereafter cited as M234).

45. M234, reel 35.

46. Thomas Henley to George Manypenny, December 4, 1856, M234, reel 35.

47. Dillon, *Fool's Gold*, pp. 341–50.

48. Hurtado, *Indian Survival*, pp. 55–71, 100–117.

49. Stephen W. Kearny to Sutter, April 7, 1847, Letters Sent by the Governors and Secretary of State of California, 1847–48, Records of the Adjutant General's Office, RG 94, National Archives Microfilm Publication M182; D. C. Goddard to A. S. Loughery, March 22, 1849, M234, reel 32; and Sutter to the secretary of the interior, May 23, 1850, M234, reel 32.

50. Hurtado, *Indian Survival,* pp. 125–48, 150–53.

51. [McKinstry], [Population Enumeration of the Sacramento Valley], November 1846, MSS. 12–13, MKP; and Sutter, "Estimate of Indian Population," December 20, 1847, MSS. 14–15, MKP.

52. Rupert Costo and Jeannette Henry Costo, *The Missions of California: A Legacy of Genocide* (San Francisco: Indian Historian Press, 1987).

John Sutter:

A Biographical Examination

Iris H. W. Engstrand

While many writers and lecturers have given detailed attention to his public career, my purpose is to present John Sutter as a human being, to look at his private life and at those traits of character that contributed to his total personality. But the task has its complications. Early biographers of Sutter (as with other well-known figures in California history) often decided in advance that their subject was a hero or a villain, and then proceeded to marshal only the evidence that would uphold their foregone conclusions. Some of these writers, moreover, mixed into the facts their own imaginary version of events. The result has been a historical literature that mixes factual reality with falsehoods and half-truths, giving rise to different and contradictory images of John Sutter.

In an attempt to separate truth from literary fantasy, I have developed a biographical portrait of John Sutter, taken from contemporary accounts, that also incorporates the results of recent scholarship. If this view seems more negative than positive, it is because I have tried to distinguish the man from the deeds for which he is best known, and to counteract the myths that have been perpetuated by several popular biographies.

First, there is the matter of Sutter's early life—fact and fiction. In this case the historian cannot rely on Sutter's own accounts, letters, or diaries—normally excellent primary sources—because he later invented for himself a suitable, more usable past than was rightfully his. As a matter of fact, Sutter was born at Kandern in the German margravate of Baden, thirteen miles north of Basel, Switzerland, on February 15, 1803, and baptized on February 23. He was the son of Johann Jakob Suter, a foreman in a paper mill whose family had been simple peasants—possibly cobblers as the surname Suter implies—who had come from and maintained ties to the village of Runenberg. His mother, Christina Wilhelmina Stober, was a clergyman's daughter from Grenzach, located farther up the Rhine River.[1] It can be surmised that John inherited his resourcefulness, his love of books, his eloquence of speech, and his gift for making friends with ease from his parents: a father who had risen above the general level of a workingman and a mother whose life centered on the activities of a pastor's family.

It is generally well known that Sutter liked to appear in uniform. Most of his portraits show him dressed as a military officer. Since the town of Kandern, where Sutter attended elementary school, was located near the only bridge over which Napoleon's armies could cross the Rhine River, Sutter grew up in a setting where soldiers, uniforms, and military pageantry were much apparent. As a result of the battle of Leipzig in October 1813, Czar Alexander of Russia, Emperor Joseph II of Austria, and King August Wilhelm of Prussia met in nearby Basel, Switzerland, on January 1, 1814, to establish headquarters for their campaign against Napoleon. During these years Kandern had its share of troops quartered in town, and their colorful military garb no doubt presented an exciting spectacle to a boy just approaching his teens. Hence it is easy to believe that Sutter's later fascination with military matters was a carry-over from this formative period in his life.[2]

Sutter left his small German village at the age of fifteen to attend school in nearby Neuchâtel, Switzerland. Subsequently he began an apprenticeship with Emanuel Thurneysen, a publisher, bookseller, and printer in Basel, a city then, as now, located on one of the foremost trading routes between Germany and France. A cultural center, Basel had been the site of a university since 1460. Yet Sutter did not succeed in the publishing and bookselling trade in Basel, and he never later showed the fascination with city life that helped shape the careers of so many young men during this period.

Rather than remain in Basel, young Sutter next moved to take a position as a clerk in a draper's shop in nearby Aarburg. There he met Anna, or Annette, Dübeld, who was to become his wife. He then moved to Annette's hometown of Burgdorf in the canton of Bern, where Annette's mother, a widow, possessed assets in the amount of 20,000 Swiss francs—a comfortable estate, though no great fortune. Following a courtship about which we can only speculate, John Sutter, by then a clerk in a grocery store, married Annette Dübeld on October 24, 1826, receiving a dowry of 2,000 francs. On the following day, October 25, the newlywed husband witnessed the birth of his first child, Johann August Sutter, Jr. Other children followed with regularity.

Despite John's residence in Burgdorf, Swiss custom dictated that the Sutter family's official hometown would remain Runenberg, some thirty miles away. In his adopted town of Burgdorf, he was considered a stranger without certain rights, and he was at a disadvantage when competing with the native businessmen for profits and social advantages.[3] John's mother-in-law, however, backed him in a dry goods firm called Johann August Suter & Co. True to a later pattern, he took on an irresponsible partner in the business who soon left him burdened with considerable debt.

During this period Sutter did spend time in the military; but he never became an officer in the "Swiss Army," a claim he later made in his "Personal Reminiscences." James Peter Zollinger, who wrote extensively on Sutter's European background, believed that Sutter had absolutely no experience with the military; but Richard Dillon, researching a biography of Sutter published in 1967, found that he actually had volunteered for the reserve corps in Bern in 1828. Within three years, by 1831, the young man had advanced to the rank of first underlieutenant of the second center company of the third battalion.[4] Yet, despite his later statements, Sutter never served in the Spanish campaign of 1823–24; nor is it likely that he fought under Charles X at Grenoble in July 1830.

While serving part-time as a military reservist, Sutter tried to make a success of his dry goods business. Not content to wait for customers to come to the Burgdorf store, he traveled the countryside "to obtain orders from farmers for cloth and yarn, thread and needles, buttons and ribbons, and all sorts of trimming and finery."[5] Handicapped by his status as a stranger, he failed to make a success of these business efforts. Indeed, the scale of Sutter's first financial failure is truly astounding. He piled up a debt of more than 50,000 francs, eventually finding himself in an impossible position. Apparently his tendency to overreach himself financially, to expand his business on borrowed funds while hoping for a miraculous upturn in his fortunes, was already pronounced long before he reached California.

By mid-May of 1834, Sutter had secretly liquidated all of his assets. Abandoning his wife and by then five children, he headed for the French port city of Le Havre with no intention of ever returning. On June 9, 1834, Sutter's creditors started bankruptcy proceedings against him, and the court issued a warrant of arrest on June 12. When his mother-in-law died six months later, she left her daughter Annette just over 25,000 francs; but this legacy remained tied up in the estate until 1862, when John Sutter finally satisfied his Swiss creditors. For more than a decade Annette Dübeld Sutter, the deserted wife and young mother, remained virtually a charity case, waiting vainly for her errant husband to rescue her from poverty and disgrace.

Coincidentally, Sutter's younger brother, Jakob Friedrich, had married Annette's sister, Marie Sophie; but this union soon came to an end. Marie Sophie divorced the younger Sutter when he turned out to be an alcoholic. Jakob, who ended up living on charity, died in 1844.[6] "Thus," as Zollinger concluded, ". . . Johann August Suter brought disgrace, misery, heart-breaks, and financial loss into the Dübeld family by many means and roads."[7]

Sutter landed in New York in July 1834 and set out immediately for the West in the company of two Germans and two Frenchmen. Eventually he arrived in St. Louis, where he met Johann August Laufkotter from Westphalia. These two adventurous newcomers to America then traveled together for more than two years. By this point Sutter had invented for himself a new personal history, featuring an enviable childhood, a military education, and a rank in the elite Swiss guard. As a result of the experience with his mendacious friend, Laufkotter has left us a rather critical account of Sutter's trading, gold mining, and smuggling activities in the Santa Fé area, and later in Westport, Missouri, where Sutter settled briefly in 1837.[8]

Benjamin D. Wilson, a fur trader in New Mexico who later moved to Los Angeles and became a respected member of that community, also accused Sutter of wrongdoing in the Santa Fé trade. Wilson, who dictated his memoirs in 1877, recorded that Sutter once approached some Germans who had brought a cargo of trade goods to Santa Fé, and offered to take their business stock southward down the Rio

Grande, where he would sell it to certain rich Mexicans for a high profit. Sutter allegedly sold the goods, returned to Santa Fé feigning illness, and reported that he had not yet had time to collect the money due. He sent Captain Saunders, head of the German party, downriver to collect the money—but Saunders found that Sutter had already received payment in full. When Saunders then returned to Santa Fé, he learned that Sutter had left his "sickbed" and was on his way back to Missouri with the proceeds.[9] The Germans made an attempt to pursue Sutter but were unable to overtake him.

For Sutter's year in Westport, Laufkotter is the principal source. Sutter represented himself as a businessman with large interests in the fledgling frontier town, and he spent freely while making his headquarters a local German saloon. Among his beneficiaries were Shawnee Indians, who worked as wage labor in building for Sutter an elaborate structure meant for a hotel—apparently his first experience with Indian employees. Among other stories, Laufkotter made frank mention of Sutter's sexual attachments with young Shawnee Indian women, who came frequently into town to seek his company. The source of his funds Sutter kept a secret, but Laufkotter leads his readers to believe that Sutter engaged in a profitable business selling whiskey illegally at the Shawnee and Delaware towns located close to Westport. Even so, at a time of general financial collapse, his speculations exceeded his income, and by the late winter of 1837–38 Sutter again prepared secretly to skip out on his debtors.[10]

Sutter departed from Westport for Oregon in April 1838, accompanying a group from the American Fur Company, and reached the Methodist Willamette mission in western Oregon on November 1. He soon sailed from the Oregon Country on the bark *Columbia* to the Hawaiian Islands, where he arrived on December 9, 1838. Gifted with a ready tongue, Sutter raised credit in the sum of $3,008.68 from the French and Greenaway Company in Honolulu to outfit his California adventure. Ten years later the French company would present him a bill, which he managed to pay with proceeds from the sale of Sacramento lots.[11]

Sutter's stay in Hawaii, his trip to the Russian colony in Alaska on the trading ship *Clementine,* his arrival in California on July 1, 1839, his acquisition of land upriver through a grant from Governor Juan Bautista de Alvarado, his purchase of Fort Ross from the Russians, and his rivalry with Mariano Guadalupe Vallejo are all developments that are well documented in California's pre-gold-rush history. We may turn from the record of events to the assessments of John Sutter's career and character that have reached the public over the years.

Before any biographer, Sutter was perhaps his own best public relations person. His letters, although seldom intimate or very personal, show him to be always polite and generally interested in what he could immediately buy or trade for whatever he could promise to deliver in the future. He did talk about his "tremendous prosperity just around the corner, all debts just about to be paid (or, anyway, next year) and a Swiss family at home, cultured, accomplished, educated up to the nines, handsome, and resourceful, and about to join him 'in four or five months' in New Helvetia."[12]

Although willing to pose as a good husband and proud father, Sutter never did send for his wife and children. The family finally reached California in January 1850, paying their way with money provided by John Sutter, Jr., the eldest son, who had joined his father on his own initiative in the fall of 1848. Heinrich Lienhard, who worked for Sutter and whose comments about Sutter are extremely insightful, had traveled to Switzerland in 1849 to arrange for the family's passage. Lienhard found Anna Sutter to be quarrelsome, and the children difficult and poorly raised. But one can hardly blame poor Mrs. Sutter for doing a less than adequate job. She did confirm for Lienhard that many of John's stories about his past were fictitious.

Probably a more serious lack of information in Sutter's own writings is the omission of any reference to Manaiki, his Hawaiian mistress who bore him several children. He is equally silent (or circumspect) regarding the various California Indian women that he kept as "personal servants." According to Lienhard, Sutter liked the younger Indian girls; when Manaiki got too old in his estimation, the patriarch of New Helvetia turned her over to one of the Hawaiians to marry.

In general, Sutter treated his Indians poorly. Those who worked at the fort all slept in one big room with a bare floor and no sanitary facilities.[13] He also supplied Indians to other Californians, as demonstrated in several letters to William Leidesdorff. For example, on April 17, 1846, he wrote: "The Indian Girl which I promised you could not come this time . . . but the next voyage you may look for her. I shall be able to send you the 8 Indians in about 6 weeks."[14] Then on May 11,

1846: "I am very sorry that it layed not in my power to send you the 10 Indians this time . . . only in harvest time you can select them, while they are all coming here to work; but by the next voyage of the launch I will send you 10 selected Indians or even 12 if you like. . . . I send two Indian Girls, of which you will take which you like the best, the *other* is for Mr. Ridley, whom I promised one longer as two year's ago. As this shall never be considered as an article of trade [I] make you a present with this girl."[15]

An interesting firsthand Indian account dictated in 1874 by Isidora, the ninety-year-old wife of Chief Solano, to one of Hubert Howe Bancroft's interviewers is particularly revealing. Isidora recalled that

> in winter when the white man came we did not know liquor, but Sutter forced the Jienguinero Indians to exchange hides for liquor, skins, fresh fish. Sutter had an Indian woman, not a Californian. She was a Canacha (Hawaiian) Indian who arrived in a boat with him. I do not like the white man much because he is a liar and a thief. . . . Sutter lied to everyone, took everything, and paid nothing.[16]

At age ninety, of course, Isidora might have had a faulty recollection. Nevertheless, as British historian John Hawgood wrote, "We find in Sutter's own writings no direct mention of his many dusky mistresses, of numerous progeny of half-breed children . . . although he did tell Pierson B. Reading (who knew exactly what he meant) to 'see that Manaiki receives her wages. . . .'"[17]

In defense of Sutter, we should recall that he did befriend many Indians. When the daughter of Anashe, a Miwok headman, was ill with measles, "Sutter spent a considerable amount of time and energy trying to cure her."[18] But, ironically, Sutter killed Raphero, the son of Maximo, another Miwok headman. When Maximo then withdrew his support from Sutter, Sutter drove him off the land.

Another pervading subject in Lienhard's study, also mentioned by others, has to do with Sutter's drinking. According to Lienhard, "Sutter was addicted to strong alcoholic drink." None of the evidence concerning Sutter's early career in Switzerland points clearly toward a drinking problem. By the time he reached Westport, however, his fondness for alcohol was very much an element in his behavior, and may already have become a major handicap to his business activities.

Once in California, the open carousing that characterized Sutter's brief stay in Westport apparently gave way to more circumspect behavior. During the early years in New Helvetia, as Sutter related, alcohol was scarce.[19] Lienhard, who arrived there in 1846, stated that for some time he "had no idea [Sutter] drank as much as he did." But on one occasion, Lienhard recorded, when Sutter had been drinking and was "in an ugly temper, [he] had thrown the dishes and plates off the table, breaking most of them. . . ." Sutter's drunken outbursts did not earn Lienhard's appreciation. "I pitied him," Lienhard wrote, "for at the time it appeared to be his worse trait, but I soon discovered . . . that he had other equally unfortunate characteristics."

During Lienhard's years at the fort, Sutter periodically indulged in alcoholic binges while keeping up a pattern of steady drinking on a day-to-day basis, a combination that typifies one form of behavior now labeled as alcoholism. As Lienhard reported, one of Sutter's "drinking sprees lasted about three days. [Yet] it was in no way extraordinary; he was never entirely sober."[20] In 1849, when Sutter was nominated for governor of California, one of his contemporaries commented, "How can a man in his senses think that responsible men would ever vote for a man like Sutter, who is drunk more than half of the time?"[21] After Mrs. Sutter and their children arrived at Sutter's Fort, however, and particularly after the family removed to Hock Farm, Sutter may have moderated his drinking behavior somewhat. According to contemporary report, however, he still attracted unfavorable notice with episodes of public drunkenness during trips away from home, whether to Sacramento, San Francisco, or other centers of gold-rush-era conviviality.

Despite his problems, Sutter worked very hard between 1840 and 1846 to build the largest and best fortified structure in California. He carried on a brisk business with Mexicans and Americans alike, corresponding frequently in Spanish and English. Many of his letters are contained in the papers of Thomas O. Larkin, U.S. consul in Monterey, a man with whom Sutter dealt frequently for supplies and other goods. Sutter's letters to Larkin talk about the good work done by "his Indians" and the high caliber of people who were arriving at the fort on the overland trail. He was known among overland immigrants for his kindness and generosity. A newspaper article in the *Daily Alta California* just before Sutter's death commented that "weary, worn, ragged . . . hungry, desolate, adrift in a strange land, they cannot have forgotten the kindly face and generous heart, the pleasant welcome and open hand . . . how the honest old Swiss Captain figuratively poured oil upon their bruises . . . and literally fed and clothed them."[22]

As the pre-gold-rush emigrants arrived, Sutter extended a hand, gave them a shelter and supplies, and sometimes put them to work. He gave relief to the survivors of the Donner Party and so many others that no one can doubt Sutter's kindness in this regard. He employed every man who asked for a job and who was prepared to stay—even those who soon proved to be worthless and helped themselves to his stores.[23] Hubert Howe Bancroft put it another way:

> Though Sutter's establishment did something to promote the influx of Amer[ican] settlers, it was in no sense beneficial to the interests of the U.S., merely fomenting filibusterism with all its unhappy results. . . . That the establishment, chiefly by reason of its situation at the foot of the mountains, was of benefit to the immigrants is true; also that Sutter treated them kindly, though not more so than a dozen others; but that he did so at a personal sacrifice, as has been so often claimed, is not true; for Sutter's letters of that time are full of self-gratulations on his lucky chance to exchange food and cattle for wagons and implements, to hire mechanics, and to have his land increased in value by the influx of settlers.[24]

After the discovery of gold, when Sutter's Fort became a depot for many thousands of gold-seekers, Sutter's luck definitely began to turn. He complained bitterly of being swindled out of his land and other property while squatters ignored his claims. His debts piled up, and in an effort to save his property he transferred some of his holdings to his son John A. Sutter, Jr. When the young Sutter had first arrived at the fort, "He found that all his father's property was at everyone's disposal, his books in chaos, and his important legal documents and maps lying about as if they were waste paper. Worse, he found that his father was in debt by at least $80,000 . . . and was using for his own purposes . . . the gold dust entrusted to him by miners for safekeeping."[25]

Marguerite Eyer Wilbur, the translator of Heinrich Lienhard's *A Pioneer at Sutter's Fort,* also wrote a "romantic biography" of Sutter subtitled *Rascal and Adventurer*. Although she often fictionalized the story, Wilbur had studied the sources enough to describe John Jr.'s reaction to his father as follows:

> He had come to the fort from Europe full of boyish ideals and hero worship for the father who had become a romantic figure and the most important man on the west coast. He had expected so much of his parent: companionship, affection, understanding. He had found, instead, a man addicted to every kind of folly; a man with frontier standards of conduct which he could not understand, and the shock of learning the truth about his father's infidelities reacted disastrously upon him. He was also gravely troubled about his parent's vindictive spirit toward him. Twice the Captain in the throes of intoxication and a flaring temper . . . had berated him for having been the cause of his forced marriage. . . .[26]

Unfortunately, the twenty-one-year-old son had little knowledge of frontier living, and he had neither the experience nor the judgment to deal with his father's debts or creditors, or to cope with the business follies committed by the senior Sutter while drunk.[27] Obviously overextended and unable to keep up with his mortgage payments, Sutter took his family to Hock Farm, a piece of property that he owned on the Feather River near Marysville.[28] He managed to save the property and lived there, albeit not in very good health, until it burned down on June 21, 1865. A year earlier the California legislature had voted him a pension of $15,000, to be paid at $250.00 per month for five years, and later he was able to get these payments renewed for another four years.

In 1871 Sutter moved to the Moravian town of Lititz, Pennsylvania, where there were medicinal springs and congenial neighbors. He presided at the Swiss Day festival in Philadelphia in 1876 and continued to petition the federal government for compensation for his lost property and alleged wrongs of the past. He told historian Hubert Howe Bancroft, when the latter visited him in Lititz, that he had "been robbed and ruined by lawyers and politicians. My men were crushed by the iron heel of civilization; my cattle were driven off by hungry gold-seekers; my fort and mills were deserted and left to decay; my lands were squatted on by overland immigrants; and, finally, I was cheated out of all my property. All Sacramento was once mine. . . ."[29]

Congress adjourned June 16, 1880, without passing a bill that would have given Sutter $50,000 for his services in the Mexican War. Two days later, on June 18, he died in his room at the Pennsylvania Hotel in Washington, D.C.[30] His faithful wife Annette died six months later, on January 19, 1881.

Sutter's contemporaries and associates expressed a variety of opinions regarding his character and abilities. In 1846 his business correspondent Thomas Larkin stated that the Swiss pioneer was "a capable man for many different offices . . . [but] much borne down by debt from the loss of two or three harvests."[31] John Bidwell, a longtime friend, never spoke ill of Sutter even though he worked closely with him for many years. After Sutter's daughter Anna Eliza had lived in California for some time, Sutter asked Bidwell to marry her to prevent her from wedding an unsuitable candidate, young Alphonse Sutter's piano teacher. Bidwell's polite refusal indicated the respect that he had for Sutter and his family.[32]

Hubert Howe Bancroft, while expressing appreciation for Sutter's kindly nature and sympathy for the misfortunes of his later years, certainly made a harsh assessment of Sutter, for he commented that Sutter's "wealth, won by good luck without business capacity, could not thus be kept under the new conditions of the flush times. . . ." Bancroft also wrote:

none of the pioneers named in this [pioneer] register has received so much praise from so many sources; few have deserved so little. . . . He was but an adventurer from the first, entitled to no admiration or sympathy. His career in N[ew] Mex[ico] was, at the best, discreditable. He came to Cal[ifornia] in the false character of an ex-capt[ain] of the French army. He was great only in his wonderful personal magnetism and power of making friends for a time of all who could be useful to him; good only in the possession of kindly impulses. His energy was a phase of his visionary and reckless enthusiasm; his executive ability did not extend beyond the skillful control of Indians and the management of an isolated trading post. Of principle, of honor, of respect for the rights of others, we find but slight trace in him. . . . There were no classes of his associates, hardly an individual, with whom he did not quarrel, or whom in his anger he did not roundly abuse. For all the favors received at the hands of Californians, he did not hesitate to turn against them, or even to arm foreigners and Indians against them, when a personal advantage seemed within his reach. . . . His only capital was money borrowed on the way to Cal[ifornia], or property obtained on credit from Californians and Russians after his arrival, all on pretenses more or less false. He never hesitated to assume any obligation for the future without regard to his ability to meet it; he rarely if ever paid a debt when due. . . .[33]

Josiah Royce, writing in his classic nineteenth-century account of California, offers an appraisal more balanced than the view put forward by Bancroft:

In character Sutter was an affable and hospitable visionary, of hazy ideas, with a great liking for popularity, and with a mania for undertaking too much. A heroic figure he was not, although his romantic position as a pioneer in the great valley made him seem so to many travelers and historians. When the gold-seekers later came, the ambitious Sutter utterly lost his head and threw away all his truly wonderful opportunities. He, however, also suffered many things from the injustice of the newcomers. He died a few years since in poverty, complaining bitterly of American ingratitude. He should undoubtedly have been better treated by most of our countrymen, but, if he was often wronged he was also often in the wrong, and his fate was the ordinary one of the persistent and unteachable dreamer. He remained to the end a figure more picturesque than manly in our California life.[34]

The Indians of northern California, especially the women, might well have spoken differently about John Sutter's affability and his "kindly nature." His kindly impulses did not always extend in their direction, and we have no record of the fate of his illegitimate children. As Professor Hurtado points out in his work on Indian survival in California, Sutter ironically shared the fate of the Indians with whom he had such a checkered career, losing his land and living his final years upon the charity of others.[35]

Sutter's Swiss-born children had their share of problems. Emil, who was partially deaf and moody as a child, committed suicide in Belgium in 1883. John Jr., unable to cope with his own and his father's business situations, fell into drinking and ill health. He finally left San Francisco for Acapulco, Mexico, in July 1850. After recovering his health and entering a long and successful marriage, he returned briefly in an attempt to collect the large amount—some $100,000—still owed him in Sacramento by Samuel Brannan and other former business partners. But John Jr. could not deal with the sharp practices of these early-day real estate speculators, and ultimately fled again to his home in Acapulco, $339 in debt, vowing that he never wanted to see Sacramento again. His sister, Anna Eliza, in 1852 overcame her father's objections and wed the piano teacher that Sutter Sr. had earlier sent away from Hock Farm. But perhaps father had known best, for the marriage ended in divorce a year later. Subsequently Anna Eliza remarried and, as Bancroft records, moved to Acapulco near her brother, John Jr., where she was still living in 1880 as the wife of Dr. Link.[36] We may think it significant that none of Sutter's children were closely in touch with him at the time of his death.

While Sutter's own accounts of his life show him as a man eager to claim credit for any success and quick to blame others for his failures, some other writers have presented his achievements in a very favorable light. As an extreme example of uncritical adulation, an enthusiastic reviewer of Julian Dana's laudatory 1935 biography of Sutter praised the book's authenticity and reported that within its pages rose "the homeric figure of a dreamer, who spun fantasies of empires, yet kept his feet close to the fertile soil as he sweated and schemed to transform his nebulous schemes into realities despite hostile Indians, jealous Mexicans and the threats of rising hordes of immigrants."[37]

Richard Dillon, whose full-length biography of Sutter first appeared in 1967, believed that even though Sutter had his weaknesses "by the score," he was "at least kindly and easy-going." While pointing out various of Sutter's character flaws, Dillon concluded that Sutter was less calculating than some of his rivals and that "his own yearnings for self-aggrandizement were checked by his kindness, prodigality and compassion." According to Dillon, Sutter was also a visionary—a colonizer who belonged "to that class of loners who preceded the first wave of men into the wilderness, far in the van of the more orthodox—and more ruthless—builders of civilization."[38]

After reexamining the evidence, we may agree today that Sutter was an energetic builder; but I do not find him kindly or compassionate to those closest to him. He was a failure as a father and as a family man. He helped many people during his Sacramento years, but he abused and disappointed quite a few others whose accounts are only beginning to be studied. No one should fail to recognize that Sutter accomplished a great deal in founding his colony of New Helvetia. A kinder, more compassionate person perhaps would not have been able to accomplish so much. We can, however, also see that his visionary qualities, like the speculative optimism always inherent in his grand plans, came linked with a strong tendency to avoid responsibility for his own errors of judgment—great and small alike—and to blame his failures on someone else.

Far from being a loner, it was one source of his many failures that Sutter always wanted to surround himself with others, and to conduct both his business and personal life in such a way as to impress his boon companions with his own ineffable greatness, no matter at what expense to those directly dependent on him. In the end, John Sutter's private life and his traits of character reveal to us that behind the public persona was an individual who failed others even more than he failed himself. Yet it is this biographical examination that enables us to see in John Sutter a more interesting figure, with all his flaws, than the mythical hero and hapless victim who has been portrayed so often in the drama of northern California's pre-gold-rush development.

Notes

1. James Peter Zollinger, "John Augustus Sutter's European Background," *California Historical Society Quarterly* 14 (1935): 30–31; and Erwin G. Gudde, "Source of the Sutter Myth," *California Historical Society Quarterly* 9 (1930): 399.

2. Albert Ferdinand Morris, though writing in a disparaging fashion, recalled Sutter exclaiming with pleasure that his military excursions with his Indian troops reminded him of his own country in "old times"; quoted in Richard Dillon, *Fool's Gold: The Decline and Fall of Captain John Sutter of California* (New York: Coward-McCann, 1967; reprint, Santa Cruz, California: Western Tanager, 1981), p. 353.

3. Zollinger, "Sutter's European Background," pp. 37–38.

4. Zollinger, "Sutter's European Background," pp. 35–36; and Dillon, *Fool's Gold,* p. 23. Dillon corresponded with Mrs. Dora Grob in Bern.

5. Zollinger, "Sutter's European Background," p. 39.

6. Zollinger, "Sutter's European Background," p. 39.

7. Zollinger, "Sutter's European Background," pp. 42–43.

8. John A. Laufkotter, *John A. Sutter, Sr., and His Grants* (Sacramento: Russell and Winterburn, 1867).

9. Doyce Nunis, "A Mysterious Chapter in the Life of John A. Sutter, *California Historical Society Quarterly* 38 (1959): 321.

10. Laufkotter, *John A. Sutter,* pp. 14–16; and Dillon, *Fool's Gold,* pp. 41–42.

11. Dillon, *Fool's Gold,* p. 72.

12. John Hawgood, "John Augustus Sutter: A Reappraisal," *Arizona and the West* 4 (Winter 1962): 351.

13. Heinrich Lienhard, *A Pioneer at Sutter's Fort, 1846–1850: The Adventures of Heinrich Lienhard,* trans. and ed. Marguerite Eyer Wilbur (Los Angeles: Calafia Society, 1941), p. 76.

14. Sutter to William A. Leidesdorff, April 17, 1846, MS. 122, Leidesdorff Collection, Henry E. Huntington Library, San Marino, California (hereafter cited as LC).

15. Sutter to William A. Leidesdorff, May 11, 1846, MS. 129, LC. On June 1, 1846, Sutter wrote that "It is all right to me that you have presented the Indian Girl to Mrs. Rae," MS. 137, LC.

16. Autobiography of Isidora recorded by Henry Cerruti and certified by Salvador Vallejo and M. A. McLaughlin, 1874, MS. 65, p. 12, Bancroft Library, University of California, Berkeley.

17. Hawgood, "John Augustus Sutter," p. 352.

18. Albert L. Hurtado, *Indian Survival on the California Frontier* (New Haven: Yale University Press, 1988), p. 215.

19. John Augustus Sutter, "Personal Reminiscences of General John Augustus Sutter," MS, Bancroft Library, University of California, Berkeley.

20. Lienhard, *A Pioneer at Sutter's Fort,* pp. 68, 75, 154. A note by editor and translator Wilbur states that "folios 141–142 of Lienhard's manuscript describing the Captain's drunken conduct have been omitted."

21. Dillon, *Fool's Gold,* p. 320.

22. *Daily Alta California* (San Francisco), May 12, 1879.

23. Hawgood, "John Augustus Sutter," p. 354.

24. Hubert Howe Bancroft, *History of California,* 7 vols. (San Francisco: History Company, 1884–1890), 5:739–40.

25. Dillon, *Fool's Gold,* p. 299.

26. Marguerite Eyer Wilbur, *John Sutter: Rascal and Adventurer* (New York: Liveright Publishing Corporation, 1949), pp. 292–93.

27. Early in 1849 John Sutter, Jr., hired Peter Hardeman Burnett, a lawyer who had recently arrived from Oregon, as his legal counsel and business agent. Burnett subdivided, advertised, and launched the sale of a large part of the estate in the Sacramento area between the fort and the embarcadero on the Sacramento River. Burnett was to receive one-fourth of the proceeds from the lots. Within six months Burnett had raised enough money from land sales to pay off the Sutters' debts, including the balance owed to the Russian-American Fur Company for the purchase of Fort Ross eight years earlier. The elder Sutter, however, became angry with his son and Burnett for creating a new city, Sacramento, which competed for trade with Sutter's own Sutterville, located on higher ground a short distance downriver. The rift was aggravated after John Sr., while drunk, signed over $20,000 worth of properties in Sutterville to some alleged friends, who made generous gifts of these lands to lure business from Sacramento. When John Jr. and his partners then attempted to counter this threat by offering similar bounties, the elder Sutter took back control of his lands from his son and ousted Burnett. See Nicholas Perkins Hardemann, *Wilderness Calling: The Hardemann Family in the American Westward Movement, 1750–1900* (Knoxville: University of Tennessee Press, 1977), pp. 203–4.

28. An article by Ruth Ward appearing on March 30, 1944, called "Old Papers Show How Sutter Lost Valuable Lands," consists of ten documents, including a bond made out by Sutter to Charles Polhemus of San Francisco on October 21, 1852, for $24,000. Another was a mortgage from Sutter and his wife Anna for $12,000 at four percent per month interest. Sutter defaulted, and the mortgage was assigned to John Q. Packard and Edward Woodruff of Marysville on July 25, 1853. Sutter was $1,558.30 behind in payments. On May 23, 1857, the property sold for $48,443.61—twelve square miles were sold for a $12,000 debt that had been compounded in three years to $33,000. See Obituary Notices, Sutter Collection, MSS. C-D 14, Bancroft Library, University of California, Berkeley (hereafter cited as SC-BL). Sutter's continuing financial problems are also evident in two letters written in French to Ferdinand Vignes at San José, dated February 13, 1852, and March 28, 1856, found in the Seaver Cen-

ter for Western History Research, Natural History Museum of Los Angeles County, Los Angeles, California. In both these letters he made promises to repay soon a sum that he had borrowed from Vignes, basing his expectations on the promise of favorable court decisions and action on his claims by Congress; "mais encore," he urged in 1856, "un peu de patience s'il vous plait."

29. Dillon, *Fool's Gold*, p. 347.

30. Dillon, *Fool's Gold*, p. 350. In the *Berkeley Gazette* of November 6, 1940, an article concerning the records held by Sutter's great-grandchildren for funeral expenses showed that undertaker Henry Lees submitted an itemized bill for "walnut casket, imitation rosewood, cost $125.00; engraved plate, $8.00; embalming $25.00; hearse $6.00 and shaving $3.00." See Obituary Notices, MSS. C-D 14, SC-BL.

31. George P. Hammond, ed., *The Larkin Papers: Personal, Business, and Official Correspondence of Thomas Oliver Larkin, Merchant and United States Consul in California,* 10 vols. (Berkeley: University of California Press, 1951–64) 4:332–33.

32. Hawgood, "John Augustus Sutter," p. 353. Unfortunately, when Engler, her suitor, was sent away, Anna Eliza attempted suicide by cutting her wrists. According to Lienhard, Sutter was in such a rage that instead of sympathy he offered her a pistol to make a good job of it; see Dillon, *Fool's Gold*, p. 329.

33. Bancroft, *History of California*, 5:739.

34. Josiah Royce, *California: From the Conquest in 1846 to the Second Vigilance Committee in San Francisco: A Study of American Character* (Boston: Houghton, Mifflin and Company, 1886; reprint, Santa Barbara: Peregrine Publishers, Inc., 1970), p. 34.

35. Hurtado, *Indian Survival*, pp. 215–17.

36. Dillon, *Fool's Gold*, pp. 327–28; John A. Sutter, Jr., *Statement Regarding Early California Experiences,* ed. Allan R. Ottley (Sacramento: Sacramento Book Collectors Club, 1943); and Bancroft, *History of California*, 5:739.

37. *Oakland Tribune,* January 6, 1935.

38. Dillon, *Fool's Gold*, p. 355.

5

John Sutter

and the Natural World

Richard White

When John Sutter sailed up the Sacramento River in 1839 and established Sutter's Fort near the juncture of the Sacramento and the
American rivers, he extended the boundaries of permanent European settlement into the Central Valley for the first time. In terms of
environmental change—in forwarding processes that continue to reshape the natural world in modern California—it was an act of some
significance. Sutter recognized that he was an agent of change. Later,
in various autobiographical accounts, he described the goals that he
originally had sought to accomplish. His were the conventional ambitions of Euro-Americans in the West. They can be summed up, fairly
simply, as first, taming the "wilderness" and establishing "civilization"; and second, transforming John Sutter into a very rich man.
Both these ambitions had environmental components. An environmental history of the Central Valley, and an idea of the basic forces
pushing environmental change in the United States, can be created by
looking at the attempts of a sometimes ridiculous, sometimes quite vi-
cious, sometimes admirable and generous Swiss adventurer to carve
out his own domain.

   Like all of us do with our own lives, and as historians do profes-
sionally with the lives of others, John Sutter took the events of his life
and shaped them into a story. In John Sutter's story, the environment
plays a critical role, not just as a setting but as an active agent. The
proper place to begin any account of Sutter and the environment is

with the story that John Sutter told about himself and the land of the Sacramento Valley.

In his so-called diary (which is less a diary than a story constructed after the fact), Sutter told how he and his party came into the Sacramento Valley which was "a Wilderness." In Yerba Buena, soon to become San Francisco, no one could even tell him how to find the entrance to the Sacramento River. It took him eight days to locate the river's mouth. Half the white men who accompanied him up the river quit his employ immediately, tired of traveling in "such a wilderness." The land was dangerous, and the Indians were "all armed & painted & looked very hostile." But after Sutter erected a fort, all of this gradually changed because of his "industry and labor." The land yielded cattle, hogs, wheat, and timber. It became "civilized," a source of wealth, and the base from which Anglo-American immigrants seized California.[1]

In his recollections William Heath Davis, who accompanied Sutter up the Sacramento in 1839, cast Sutter's settlement in terms of this same transformation. Davis remembered Sutter's nine-gun salute amidst "large number of deer, elk, and other animals on the plains . . . the howls of wolves and coyotes, and the immense flocks of waterfowl." Writing later, he realized that this was the "first echo of civilization in the primitive wilderness so soon to become populated and developed into a great agricultural and commercial center."[2]

What is important about the story that Sutter told about the land is how conventional it is; for this local story by and about Sutter, in fact, merely mirrors our national story of progress. Sutter had enough sense in telling his story to wrap it up within the larger success of the Anglo-American occupation of California and the gold rush. He took credit for the future. He made himself part of the larger story that the American people tell about themselves and their land. And indeed, Sutter—as did the Anglo-Americans who followed him—knew the proper plot of this story before he ever stepped ashore, onto the land that would be Sacramento. When Sutter came upriver in 1839, he brought the cultural categories necessary to tell the appropriate story just as certainly as he brought his saws, axes, and guns. What he had in his head determined how he would interpret what he did with his hands.

Sutter knew that western American history, properly told, had to be a story of wilderness conquered, "unworthy" rivals (Mexicans and

Indians) overcome, and progress ensured. When we commemorate Sutter, in effect we collectively validate this story of the transformation of a wilderness to real estate, of nature into a modern, prosperous, expanding city. It is this belief in progress, this sense of an ultimate happy resolution, that has shaped the way that Sutter and—at least until recently—most of us have perceived and organized the history of environmental change.

And yet, embedded within the Sutter story of progress and success is another story, a story of failure. Sutter himself was, in the end, a personal failure: a terrible businessman, a drunk, a miserable father and husband, and, by our definitions, probably a child molester. He was ruthless; but he was even a failure in his ruthlessness, for he was never ruthless enough for gold-rush society. Lurking within Sutter's story of progress is a hint of a price to be paid for it, the price that progress demands. Sutter's story makes the price personal. But there was also another price, and that was the price paid by the land itself.

To construct an environmental history of the Central Valley that reflects both change and the price of change—rather than simply repeating the conventional progression from wilderness to civilization—it is necessary to deconstruct the story of success that Sutter ambiguously told. We must dismantle it and reconstruct a different, more complicated setting and story from Sutter's own experiences. Let us start, as we must, with the so-called wilderness that John Sutter supposedly confronted.

Wilderness is a mutable cultural category, one that changes over time. In the purest sense of this term, wilderness is land unshaped by human actions. Humans may live in wilderness, but when they do so, they live by means of what nature offers instead of what they compel nature to produce by their own labor. When James Zollinger, Sutter's early biographer, described the land as "unclaimed primeval forests and savannahs" inhabited by "untamed savages," he was summarizing the nineteenth century's cultural category of wilderness.[3]

Taken purely in a descriptive sense, however, there was precious little primeval wilderness in the Sacramento Valley and the bordering foothill region in 1839. Indians had shaped the land that Sutter found, and fire was their major tool. Indians set fires as a hunting technique, to thin brush and promote the growth of grasses whose seed they gathered, and to prepare land for the wild tobacco seeds that they planted. Although tule elk, antelope, and deer are browsers, burning also benefited these animals—first, by keeping brush in an early and more palatable stage of succession; second, by encouraging greater growth of grasses on which they depend in the critical late winter and early spring period; and, finally, by apparently increasing the production of acorns (which both the Indians and the deer ate) in the interior live oaks and blue oaks. Deer particularly are an animal of environmental edges between forest and grassland, and deer thrived in the young brush that fires maintained in the chaparral of the foothills. In the Sierra, hunters who set fires during summer expeditions appear to have thinned mature trees, particularly on ridges, and to have killed seedlings. These light ground fires favored the yellow (or ponderosa) pine. Mature yellow pines are fire resistant and need fire to help prepare seedbeds and to discourage shade-tolerant trees.[4]

Nor, no matter what definition we give to the problematic word *savages,* were the Plains Miwok, Valley Yokuts, and other native peoples whom Sutter encountered "untamed savages." Indians had lived in the region for thousands of years. Indeed, Indians had occupied the very site of Sutter's Fort from 2,000 to 3,000 years before Sutter arrived, and Sutter's domains had been part of the most densely populated region of Indian California. These Indians were quite familiar with Europeans and European cultures by the time Sutter met them. Among the "untamed savages" who greeted him were ex-neophytes from San José, some of whom spoke Spanish and professed Christianity.[5]

When Sutter and his biographers wrote that he was bringing civilization to the Central Valley, they meant white European civilization. For them the term *civilization* could have virtually no other meaning. Just as existing cultural categories led Sutter and his biographers to see the land as a wilderness and Indians as untamed savages, so it made the arrival of civilization equal the conquest of the land by whites. Yet, initially, a simple show of hands among the conquerors would have revealed precious few white ones at Sutter's Fort. Sutter was himself European—German Swiss—although he had resided in Missouri for many years. Of the party that accompanied him, several were Europeans—a Belgian, a German, and an Irishman—ten (eight men and two women) were Hawaiians (or Kanakas as many people then called them), and one was an Indian boy whom Sutter had bought en route to California from the Wind River rendezvous in the Rocky Mountains. Many of the whites who had accompanied Sutter this far left immediately. Although others eventually took their place, Sutter relied largely on nonwhites—Indians and Hawaiians—for labor and the defense of his fort. The everyday work of conquering "wilderness" for European "civilization" was in the hands of non-Europeans. And from the Polynesian huts first built on the site to the Polynesian dress apparently partially adopted by local Indians, the signs of a more complex cultural mixing were everywhere present.[6]

Looking at Sutter's early settlement, what we find then is that the categories used to organize the story—wilderness, "savages", "white"—are much more problematic than they might seem. Like all cultural categories, when applied to an actual world, they tend to blur and alter. Sutter was not entering a "wilderness," but neither was he entering a stable Indian world. The world created by the Miwok and Yokuts was already in the midst of vast environmental changes when Sutter arrived.

The sources of this change were part of a larger process of ecological imperialism, as the historian Alfred Crosby has called it, that was transforming the planet between the sixteenth and nineteenth centuries. Sutter was an ecological invader, but he was not the first. The Spanish—or rather a few European Spanish and far more people of mixed Indian, African, and European ancestry—were the advance agents of ecological invasion and transformation in California. It was they who first introduced into the region domesticated animals, agricultural plants, and unfamiliar diseases from the Mediterranean world. But the invasion that they launched was not fully under their control. They purposefully brought horses, cattle, and sheep; but they also introduced rats and other less welcome exotics. They purposefully introduced wheat, fruit trees, and corn; but they could not keep out the various weeds that accompanied these plants. And though they benefited from the newly introduced diseases that decimated Indians, they did not introduce them here on purpose.

Indians, in the end, were the major victims of these changes, but it is wrong to see them only as victims. They initially welcomed many of the invaders and helped them spread. In the early nineteenth century, long before Sutter arrived, Miwok and Yokuts men had begun raiding the coastal missions and ranchos for horses. They used them to hunt antelope and elk, and they also ate the horses themselves. Some of these horses escaped, and wild horse herds became established in the San Joaquin Valley.[7]

With the horses, too, came less obvious changes. Horses, and later cattle driven inland from the missions and ranchos, carried with them, either in their excrement or mixed with their feed, the seeds of new plants introduced accidentally by the Spanish as weeds in the oat and wheat fields of the missions. Late-nineteenth-century California Indians insisted that they had always gathered the seeds of wild oats (*Avena fatua*), but wild oats were, in fact, an introduction. The first Indians that Frémont met as he descended into the valley in 1844 were gathering the seeds of filaree (*Eròdium*), and Frémont saw large stands of the plant later as he passed through the San Joaquin Valley. It, too, was a Spanish introduction, as were the wild ryes (*Élymus* spp. and *Lòlium* spp.) that Indians quickly adopted as food.[8]

Horses not only brought these plant invaders, but also helped ensure their success. Herds of horses, and later sheep and cattle, trampled and grazed the native perennial bunch grasses much more heavily than did native browsers. Not having evolved under this kind of intense grazing pressure, the perennial grasses lost ground both to native annuals and also to the introduced grasses that had evolved in tandem with European grazers. Such changes would quicken dramatically with the increases in livestock during the 1850s. Although the basic staples of the Indian diet—acorns, grass seeds, and wild game, supplemented by salmon—remained the same as before the coming of the Spanish, horses and exotic grasses had begun to make changes both in human diets and the landscape.[9]

What the Miwok, Yokuts, Nisenan, and neighboring peoples did not welcome was disease. During the long, slow migration through arctic regions, the hunters and gatherers who were ancestors of American Indians apparently lost most of the diseases of the Old World. The combination of the cold northern regions and the isolation of small hunting groups acted as a disease filter. And with the closing of the Bering Straits, the migrants were cut off from the disease pools of Asia, Europe, and Africa. In the western hemisphere, the lateness in creating cities and the lack of domestic animals—which often serve as hosts to diseases that affect humans—slowed the evolution of diseases. This relatively disease-free environment, however, served as a time bomb when Europeans and Africans introduced old-world diseases. Native Americans had no resistance. Unlike Europe, Africa, and Asia, where the most vulnerable had been culled from the population for millennia and where most adults had survived smallpox, measles, and other common epidemic infections in childhood, North and South America were virgin soil. And in the so-called virgin-soil epidemics they died by the millions.[10]

Epidemics ravaged and destroyed California coastal Indians and almost certainly had an impact on the interior in the late eighteenth and early nineteenth centuries, but the first clear record of a devastating epidemic in the Sacramento Valley came in 1833 when Hudson's Bay Company trappers brought malaria from Oregon into the swampy lands of the Central Valley. In August of 1833 John Work of the Hudson's Bay Company, whose own brigade of fur hunters unwittingly spread the disease in all likelihood, described villages on the lower Feather River that had been "populous and swarming with inhabitants" in January and February as then "almost deserted & having a desolate appearance." The few "wretched Indians who remain," Work recorded, ". . . are lying apparently unable to move."[11] Infected anopheles mosquitoes had spread malaria, and approximately 20,000 Indians died. When Sutter arrived, travelers could still see collapsed houses filled with skeletons and abandoned village sites littered with skulls and bones.

The death toll did not end with the first malaria epidemic. Venereal disease was widespread in the valley by the early 1840s, and in 1842 Sutter himself described "great sickness and diseases among the Indian tribes and great number of them dying. . . ."[12] In 1847 a second fatal epidemic—probably measles—struck the villages of the Upper Sacramento particularly hard. In all, between 1830 and 1847 the Indians of the Central Valley were in the midst of a massive population decline brought about by diseases, Mexican raids, and invasion of their lands. Their population dropped during these years by about 75 percent.[13]

These diseases not only opened up the valley to invasion, but they also had lingering effects on the landscape. The Sacramento Delta region, along with the lower courses of the Cosumnes, Mokelumne, Calaveras, Stanislaus, and Tuolumne rivers, probably had the highest population density of any region in aboriginal California. Not only did the native population fall drastically from malaria; but once malaria had been introduced, it became endemic and in effect shut off many of the abundant resources of this region to survivors by preventing resettlement. The Indians who confronted Sutter had seen their villages turned to graveyards and their most productive lands turned to pestilential wastes by the very people who thought of themselves as bringing civilization to a wilderness. The Spanish, British, and Anglo-Americans may not have found a wilderness, but in places they unintentionally created one.[14]

As an ecological invader, Sutter was only participating in an ongoing process. The real innovation that he brought to the shaping of the Central Valley revolved around his second ambition: making a great deal of money. Sutter thought of himself largely as a farmer. He sold wheat and cattle, and part of his obligation to the Russians for the purchase of their establishment at Fort Ross and Bodega Bay had to be paid in wheat, peas, and beans. But, in fact, Sutter sold everything for which he could find a market, including such natural products as brandy from wild grapes, salmon, lumber, elk, and deer tallow. In what late-twentieth-century capitalism regards, in another sense, as "natural"—that everything is for sale, and that the market is the final arbiter of value—lay the seeds of great environmental change. Through his various enterprises Sutter did two things. First, he turned nature into a commodity: not just something to be used, but something to be bought and sold. And, second, he took the creatures that were native to a small set of adjoining ecosystems within the valley and made them creatures of the biosphere.

We may think of this process in terms of energy production and energy consumption. Within a recurring natural cycle, plants and animals obtained in the Central Valley the energy that they needed to live. In time, whether by being eaten or by dying and decaying, they surrendered this energy to other plant and animal inhabitants of the valley. But Sutter's activities interrupted the cycle. Made into commodities and consumed elsewhere, plants and animals from this locality ended up yielding the energy in their possession far from the Central Valley.

Both commodification and the linkage of California's Central Valley to national and international markets represented major changes with major repercussions.[15] Historical writers have made it something of a convention to describe Sutter and his fort as feudal, as a self-sufficient outpost holding the surrounding region in subjugation. And, indeed, there was much production for only local consumption; but what is missed in such descriptions is the larger truth of Sutter's Fort as an outpost of the worldwide market economy. The fort's linkage with this far-reaching economic network, not its isolation, is the most important point. Indeed, anyone reading the journal of Sutter's Fort, the New Helvetia Diary, should be struck by the extent to which this site was, above all, a transit point for people and commodities. What the diary records is movement. It records who comes in and who departs—"started D. Martin for lumber . . . arrived Perry and Wyman from below with cattle . . . arrived Salinez with a band of Mares from Napa." It records the movement of goods.[16]

The barest outline of Sutter's operations reveals how far his ties with the world economy stretched. He expanded his enterprise by buying (on credit) the Russian establishments at Bodega Bay and Fort Ross, a purchase that kept him in debt for years. He armed his Indian soldiers with flintlocks that Napoleon had abandoned during his retreat from Moscow in 1812. To pay the Russians, Sutter sent them the bulk of his wheat production. And so Sacramento wheat fed Russians in Alaska. To pay other debts, he sold Indian orphans in the Bay area and leased out Indian labor from tributary villagers. Sutter also held office under the Mexican Republic, thus linking Sutter's Fort with Mexico City. He traded beaver with the Hudson's Bay Company in Oregon, whose officers took orders from London and marketed the beaver in Europe and China. And he welcomed Anglo-American immigrants from the eastern United States, who brought to New Helvetia a large array of craft skills that Sutter turned to the production of marketable goods. From Sutter's small enterprise on the Sacramento and American rivers, lines of communication and migration went out to Polynesia, Central America, Europe, Alaska, Russia, Asia, and eastern North America.[17]

Sutter's debt and his involvement in world markets meant that new pressures shaped the fate of living things along the Sacramento. Sutter sought to reshape the valley into a form that would yield him the maximum profit. This effort helped some species—in the sense of increasing their numbers—and it hurt others in the sense of decreasing them. On the whole, it hurt native species; it aided exotic or introduced species. By the early 1840s, Charles Wilkes, the naval officer in charge of the first United States expedition to explore the area, reported a decline in game south of the Feather River because of hunting by Hudson's Bay Company trappers and Sutter's own activities.[18]

There is, however, an apparent anomaly here. Why, if Sutter found a way to profit from beaver, salmon, and elk as well as cattle, did he not seek to conserve and increase the numbers of beaver, salmon, and elk as well as horses, cattle, and sheep? The answer is that because the wild animals were not domesticated, even to the meager standards that a California cow was domesticated, the wild animals became commodities or property only after they were dead. Thus, although the New Helvetia Diary can sanguinely record in 1848 that "Wyma chief Shekele, [was] flogged for killing cattle,"[19] it would have been incomprehensible to Sutter if the Miwok had flogged him for killing elk or beaver or salmon. These natural creatures, so he understood, were free to the taker. In this system, wild animals had no value while living; only their death created value. By dying, a cow or steer deprived Sutter of property; a deer or beaver by dying seemingly deprived no one of anything.

This was not, of course, the only way to organize the world, and the Indians surrounding Sutter and working for Sutter inhabited, in a sense, a different universe. Of course, they, too, killed animals and modified nature; but the Miwok or Yokuts people would have agreed with a Nomlaki Indian who told an ethnographer, "Everything in this world talks, just as we are now—the trees, rocks, everything. But we cannot understand them, just as the white people do not understand Indians." Indians lived in a world inhabited by other persons: other-than-human persons whose lives had value, and which they surrendered only under certain conditions. It was a world full of the daily rituals necessary for the deer to consent to die, the salmon to migrate, the oaks to yield acorns.[20]

Killing in the Indian world was a necessary act if humans were to live, but animals who were killed were not commodities. They were persons endowed with power who must be shown due respect. After killing particularly powerful animals—bears, eagles, or falcons—a hunter would bring the body home, lay it on a blanket, and have a little feast in its honor. This was necessary to show the animal respect and appease its spirit.[21]

Sutter was thus changing the human relation to the environment in the Central Valley. He was changing the relationship of human beings to other living things by imposing a newly dominant system in which wild plants and animals, worthless while living, became valuable when dead, and domesticated plants and animals became property. Simply put, Sutter was delivering the valley environment to the sway of the market. It was as though the valley was no more than a commercial property to let; and the lessors, Sutter and the Anglo-Americans who would follow, were willing to modify the property to suit any paying client.

Each modification, however, brought unintended consequences. When the market wanted gold, mining debris would fill the valley's rivers and increase destructive floods across the lands; when it wanted cattle, overgrazing and the introduction of exotic species would destroy the native grasses. Because potentially the land could be used for many things, the demands of the market produced a kaleidoscope of changes in the landscape of the valley: from wheat fields to orchards, to rice, to subdivisions, to business parks. The seeds—or rather the mechanism—of these transformations lay within Sutter's Fort when he was sending off 289 1/2 fanegas of wheat to the Russians or shipping forty-seven hogsheads of salted salmon to merchant Nathan Spear at Yerba Buena.[22]

By emphasizing Sutter's role in linking the Central Valley to the wider world, in transforming the relationship between human beings and other living things within it, and in accelerating the changes that would transform its ecological communities, I have neglected the sense in which Sutter and his operations also became a part of the valley, enmeshed in its existing natural patterns. One way to approach this relationship is in terms of boundaries. In any human environment, our sense of boundary and distance is as much perceptual as natural. The familiar is near; the exotic is far, no matter what their measurable distance. My wife and I, for example, have recently moved from Salt Lake City to Seattle. Our California friends—in Sacramento, Los Angeles, and San Francisco—have had a uniform reaction: they think it's great that we are going to be so much closer. Now unless I've missed some recent tectonic plate movements, Salt Lake City is roughly 750 miles from San Francisco; Seattle is 810. But to Californians, planet Utah (as new migrants to the state sometimes refer to it) floats off in its own solar system, while Californians regard Seattle as a San Francisco suburb with fir trees.

Indians had perceptually bounded the Central Valley in their own way. An Indian boy whom Sutter had delegated to guide John Charles Frémont toward the south deserted Frémont and his men at the Stanislaus River because, Frémont thought, he was "alarmed at the many streams which we were rapidly putting between him and the village."[23] Whatever it might have been, the native boundary reached by the Indian boy still continued to exist in 1844 within the other boundaries that Sutter had imposed on the land.

The boundary most important to Sutter was his grant itself. In 1841 the Mexican government gave him the New Helvetia grant of eleven square leagues (48,818 acres), which a second grant—the so-called Sobrante grant later disallowed by the U.S. government—extended to 33 square leagues or 229 square miles. Sutter, in turn, granted parts of this area to others in order to fulfill the conditions of his grant by settling twelve families on the land. But in the years that Sutter dominated the lower Sacramento Valley, this attempt to turn land into real estate and to govern its private use through public enforcement was relatively weak. Property lines would later be a major influence on how humans shaped particular parts of the valley, but they neither determined how Sutter used the land nor, when the gold rush occurred, did these lines act as much of a barrier to others seeking to use the land.[24]

In his attempt to make money from the land, John Sutter moved far beyond the princely estate that the Mexican government had given him. Yet, as much as Sutter changed the environment of the Central Valley, he could come nowhere near managing it completely. Sutter shaped the land; but the land, in turn, shaped his endeavors. The hydraulic systems of the valley, the cycles of rainy season, snow melt, and summer drought, for example, constantly interfered with his plans. Charles Wilkes clearly misgauged the valley's potential when he proclaimed a large part of it "undoubtedly barren and unproductive, and must for ever remain so,"[25] but he was correct when he pointed out that the combination of aridity and flooding created serious obstacles for farming. The best land was often underwater during critical parts of the growing season, and the uplands that did not flood were liable to drought. Sutter repeatedly lost his crops to drought. He came to recognize that only by altering the natural plumbing of the valley could he make it into prime agricultural land. The milldam for the gristmill that he was erecting five miles above the fort would double for irrigation, watering, in Sutter's words, "an immense quantity of land which will be worth $25- pr. acre."[26]

This same obstinacy of water also interfered with Sutter's livestock raising. After his purchases from the Russians, he had roughly 4,500 cattle, 1,500 horses and mules, 2,000 sheep, and an unknown number of hogs (which he kept on the Sacramento, four miles below the fort). He moved his cattle forty-five miles north of the fort to Hock Farm above the Feather River. He did so partially to keep them out of his fields, and partially to keep them out of the hands of his creditors; but he also wanted to keep them out of the Sacramento alluvial plain when it flooded during the rainy season. Because the Feather River poured such a large quantity of water into the Sacramento, flooding was much worse below the juncture of those two rivers than above. The Sutter Buttes marked both the northern edge of his grant and apparently the upper boundary of his prime wintering grounds.[27]

There was no such correspondence between Sutter's land and his sources of timber. To build on the scale that he desired, Sutter needed timber of a better quality than the valley and adjacent foothill lands could provide. Neither the oaks nor the digger pine with its curved trunk and branches formed suitable building materials, and so Sutter stretched the environmental borders of his enterprise twenty-five miles up the American River in search of yellow pine. Currently, you begin to find large numbers of drought-resistant digger pines when you travel roughly seventeen to twenty miles toward the mountains from Sutter's Fort, reaching the foothills at an elevation over 500 feet. At about twenty-five miles, beginning at an elevation of approximately 1,500 feet, you encounter yellow pine. Sutter, however, needed not just pine, but pine near a river that might carry the trees downstream in rafts to his establishment. And when he planned his mill, he needed a mill site on a river that could power his saws. Here he chose doubly badly. That James Marshall discovered gold at the Coloma site rendered all Sutter's plans superfluous, but it is hard to see how he could have moved either saw logs or finished lumber economically from the mill at Coloma in any case.[28]

Timber and cattle thus formed the boundaries of Sutter's domain.

Their natural requirements shaped what he did and where he did it, but even here we must remember that these requirements were not purely natural; for the natural requirements of cattle and trees were always mixed with the necessity of marketing them as commodities. Natural systems, tending to bound and localize, felt the enormous pressures of the market that sought to expand and mix.

The importance of these natural boundaries has faded in the century and a half since the demise of Sutter's little empire. Present-day Sacramento occupies the same place that Sutter inhabited a century and a half ago; but it requires a considerable act of the imagination to reconstruct his physical and perceptual world. Remnants of the older natural and human world that Sutter knew still remain visible—at least on smog-free days—but it is a world where the boundaries have constantly grown less and less distinct. The Sacramento Valley no longer depends on Sierra timber; most cattle come in from outside. Even water, with the rivers rearranged as part of the world's most elaborate environmental plumbing scheme, and with California always looking enviously at the water of its neighbors, no longer bounds a natural system in the sense that it did in Sutter's day.

And yet in response to this blurring of boundaries—this movement, spearheaded by Sutter, to make all of nature a commodity to be shipped wherever the demand is greatest and the price is highest—has come a countermovement to relocalize. This movement is still relatively weak. The creation of national parks is an ambiguous sign of it. National parks are set aside from normal development, and if nature is still a commodity to be consumed by tourists, it is at least a commodity that has to be consumed in place and cannot be carried away. Attempts to preserve remnant habitat, preserve vanishing species, or recreate zones of natural environmental diversity: all of these efforts are parts of an attempt to relocalize, to establish boundaries against the market that seeks not diversity but homogeneity.

The talk that Sacramento is becoming more and more like Los Angeles is usually voiced now as a criticism rather than as praise. Surely such criticism would have been unintelligible to Sutter or to the civic boosters who followed him for a century or more. For wasn't growing bigger, more populous, and richer the point? Wasn't this what Sutter's story was about? Any other conclusion would question the progress that Sutter made the theme of his story. And so perhaps today, in a way impossible to conceive until recently, the story of Sutter and his land—his New Helvetia empire—takes on meanings that it lacked for earlier generations in Sacramento. The land bounded Sutter and contained him, even as he struggled to break those boundaries and eliminate virtually all that was distinctive about the place. And now he is remembered not only as the prophet of progress that he imagined himself, but also as a man who entered a wondrous and distinctive world, a natural world now virtually gone. As we all understand, many people living amidst prosperity and "progress" are now trying to save remnants of this natural world. It is a world upon which, in a spirit very different than John Sutter's, they look back with nostalgia and longing.

Notes

1. Johann August Sutter, *The Diary of Johann August Sutter* (San Francisco: Grabhorn Press, 1932), pp. 5–6, 56.

2. William Heath Davis, *Seventy-five Years in California: Recollections and Remarks by One Who Visited These Shores in 1831, and Again in 1833, and Except When Absent on Business Was a Resident from 1838 until the End of a Long Life in 1909,* ed. Harold A. Small, 3d ed. (San Francisco: J. Howell Books, 1967), p. 16.

3. James Peter Zollinger, *Sutter: The Man and His Empire* (New York: Oxford University Press, 1939), p. 69. Raymond Dasmann's pioneering work *The Destruction of California* (New York: Macmillan, 1966) demonstrated the importance of environmental change in California history. Other regional accounts of the demographic and ecological impact of European expansion in North America include William Cronon, *Changes in the Land: Indians, Colonists, and the Ecology of New England* (New York: Hill and Wang, 1983); Albert E. Cowdrey, *This Land, This South: An Environmental History* (Lexington: University Press of Kentucky, 1983); Dan Louie Flores, "Islands in the Desert: An Environmental Interpretation of the Rocky Mountain Frontier" (Ph.D. diss., Texas A & M University, 1978); Terry G. Jordan and Matti Kaups, *The American Backwoods Frontier: An Ethnic and Ecological Interpretation* (Baltimore: The Johns Hopkins University Press, 1989); Timothy Silver, *A New Face on the Countryside: Indians, Colonists, and Slaves in South Atlantic Forests, 1500–1800* (New York: Cambridge University Press, 1990); and Richard White, *Land Use, Environment, and Social Change: The Shaping of Island County, Washington* (Seattle: University of Washington Press, 1980). Regarding the growth of

environmental history in relation to the American West, see especially Richard White, "American Environmental History: The Development of a New Historical Field," *Pacific Historical Review* 54 (August 1985): 297–335; and Donald Worster, *Under Western Skies: Nature and History in the American West* (New York: Oxford University Press, 1992).

4. Henry T. Lewis, *Patterns of Indian Burning in California: Ecology and Ethnohistory,* Ballena Press Anthropological Papers no. 1 (Ramona, California: Ballena Press, 1973), pp. 17–23, 55, 72–73; Elna S. Bakker, *An Island Called California: An Ecological Introduction to Its Natural Communities* (Berkeley: University of California Press, 1984), p. 210; James R. Sweeney, *Responses of Vegetation to Fire: A Study of the Herbaceous Vegetation Following Chaparral Fires,* University of California Publications in Botany 28, no. 4 (Berkeley: University of California Press, 1956), pp. 169–73; Stephen J. Pyne, *Fire in America: A Cultural History of Wildland and Rural Fires* (Princeton: Princeton University Press, 1982), pp. 38, 413–15; and R. S. Rossi, "History of Cultural Influences on the Distribution and Reproduction of Oaks in California," pp. 7–18, *Ecology, Management, and Utilization of California Oaks,* ed. T. R. Plumb, USDA Forest Service General Technical Report PSW-44 (Washington, D.C.: Government Printing Office, 1980).

5. William H. Olsen, *Archeological Investigations at Sutter's Fort Historical Monument* (Sacramento: Department of Natural Resources, May 1961), p. 45; and Davis, *Seventy-Five Years in California,* pp. 144, 171. For a map of Indian population densities, see Lewis, *Patterns of Indian Burning in California,* p. 87.

6. Charles Wilkes, *Narrative of the United States Exploring Expedition during the Years 1838, 1839, 1840, 1841, 1842,* 5 vols. (Philadelphia: Lea and Blanchard, 1845), 5:180.

7. Albert L. Hurtado, *Indian Survival on the California Frontier* (New Haven: Yale University Press, 1988), p. 34. On Indian raids, see George Phillips, "Commerce in the Valley: Indian-White Trade in Mexican California" (Paper presented at the American Historical Association Meeting, December 1983); and Sutter, *Diary,* p. 4.

8. Donald Jackson and Mary Lee Spence, eds., *The Expeditions of John Charles Frémont,* 3 vols. (Urbana: University of Illinois Press, 1970–73), 1:649; Robert F. Heizer and Albert B. Elsasser, *The Natural World of the California Indians* (Berkeley: University of California Press, 1980), p. 38; Bakker, *An Island Called California,* p. 168; Philip A. Munz, *A California Flora, with Supplement* (Berkeley: University of California Press, 1968), pp. 143–45, 1504–6, 1509–10; and Sacramento County Office of Education, *The Outdoor World of the Sacra-*

mento Region, Field Guide Edition (Sacramento: Sacramento County Office of Education, 1975), pp. 38, 77.

9. Bakker, *An Island Called California,* pp. 168–69. The environmental change in California's grasslands is described most fully in Dasmann, *The Destruction of California,* pp. 59–74.

10. Alfred W. Crosby, *Ecological Imperialism: The Biological Expansion of Europe, 900–1900* (New York: Cambridge University Press, 1986), pp. 285–86.

11. John Work, quoted in Sherburne F. Cook, *The Epidemic of 1830–33 in California and Oregon,* University of California Publications in Archaeology and Ethnology 43, no. 3 (1955): 316–20.

12. Sutter, *Diary,* p. 41.

13. On the decline of the Indian population, see Hurtado, *Indian Survival,* 46; Cook, *The Epidemic of 1830–33,* pp. 303–25; Heinrich Lienhard, *A Pioneer at Sutter's Fort, 1846–1850: The Adventures of Heinrich Lienhard,* trans. and ed. Marguerite Eyer Wilbur (Los Angeles: Calafía Society, 1941), p. 99; Sherburne F. Cook, *The Population of the California Indians, 1769–1970* (Berkeley: University of California Press, 1976), p. 12; John A. Sutter et al., *New Helvetia Diary: A Record of Events Kept by John A. Sutter and His Clerks at New Helvetia, California, from September 9, 1845, to May 25, 1848* (San Francisco: Grabhorn Press, 1939), August 13, 1847, p. 70; and Wilkes, *Narrative,* 5:181–83.

14. Cook, *The Population of the California Indians,* p. 8.

15. Zollinger, *Sutter,* p. 103.

16. Sutter et al., *New Helvetia Diary,* September 16 and 24, 1845, October 12, 1845, pp. 2–5, 8.

17. Sutter, *Diary,* pp. 3, 12–13, 16–17; Hurtado, *Indian Survival,* p. 46; and Zollinger, *Sutter,* p. 126.

18. Wilkes, *Narrative,* 5:183–84.

19. Sutter, *New Helvetia Diary,* March 23, 1848, p. 125.

20. Heizer and Elsasser, *Natural World,* p. 210.

21. Edward W. Gifford, *Miwok Moieties,* University of California Publications in American Archaeology and Ethnology 12, no. 4 (Berkeley: University of California Press, 1916), p. 145. Also see Edward W. Gifford, *Miwok Cults,* University of California Publications in American Archaeology and Ethnology 18, no. 3 (Berkeley: University of California Press, 1926), pp. 391–408.

22. Sutter, *New Helvetia Diary*, December 4, 1845, p. 15.

23. Donald Jackson and Mary Lee Spence, eds., *The Expeditions of John Charles Frémont*, 3 vols. (Urbana: University of Illinois Press, 1970–73), March 27, 1844, 1:660.

24. Zollinger, *Sutter*, pp. 89, 110–11, 146, 188–89, 317.

25. Wilkes, *Narrative*, 5:193.

26. Zollinger, *Sutter*, pp. 227–29.

27. Zollinger, *Sutter*, pp. 99, 108. Wilkes apparently did not include the Russian animals in his estimate; see Wilkes, *Narrative*, 5:179. On flooding of the Sacramento River, see Wilkes, *Narrative*, 5:157.

28. Zollinger, *Sutter*, pp. 163–64, 225. On the digger pine and yellow pine, see Bakker, *An Island Called California*, pp. 123–24, 185, 197; and John C. Williams and Howard C. Monroe, *Natural History of Northern California* (Dubuque, Iowa: Kendall/Hunt Publishing Company, 1976), pp. 282–84, 290–91. Later experiments in rafting pine logs down the American River invariably ended in disaster, due to the stream's rapid flow and rocky configuration before it reaches the valley floor.

6

John Sutter:

Prototype for Failure

Patricia Nelson Limerick

A few years ago, during a visit to Sacramento, my husband and I took a tour of Sutter's Fort. In one room of the fort, a staff person undertook to instruct us on the subject of John Sutter's personal life. "Sutter had a common-law Hawaiian wife," we were informed, "but he dropped her and brought his Swiss wife to California." Receiving this news, one woman in the group was moved to exclaim, "Men! They never change."

"Men! They never change"—that is one viable interpretation of the meaning of John Sutter for our times. Sutter is often referred to as the "Father of California." If Sutter did not, in literal fact, father California, that failure cannot be blamed on any lack of trying. With his Hawaiian mistress and his many encounters with Indian women and with Indian girls, Sutter did not spend his time cursing his luck for having been born too early for the sexual revolution of the 1960s. In these matters of personal behavior, behavior dampened but not ended by the later arrival of the wife whom he had abandoned in Switzerland in 1834, Sutter seems distinctly modern.

Over the last century and a half, Americans have used two extremely effective methods to dehumanize the people of the western past. The more commonly recognized method is to make historical figures seem worse than they were—to cast Indians as brutal savages, or Mexicans as cruel *bandidos,* or white settlers as uniformly ruthless pillagers of people and places. But there is another, equally effective method that works by the opposite approach. You can dehumanize historical figures just as effectively if you portray them as better than they were. The noble pioneer, selfless servant in the cause of bringing civilization and advancing progress, endurer of hardship in the service of the common good: this is one of the best mechanisms available for taking an extremely interesting human being, and making him or her into a one-dimensional bore.

For decades that was the unhappy fate of John Sutter. In life he was one of the more interesting human beings on the planet, but in death he became a bore. Those who did Sutter this disservice did not, of course, intend to injure him. Moreover, it is important to note that he spent his last years acting as his own nineteenth-century image-maker and spin-doctor, and thereby making his own contribution to this curious campaign to paint a vivid life in dull colors. When the campaign succeeded, Sutter's rich and revealing story shrank to a thin, pious parable about a man who stood at the gate of Mexican California, who welcomed Anglo-Americans as they came over the Sierra, who sponsored the discovery of gold, and who thereby made California prosper while he watched his own empire disappear in a tidal wave of gold-seekers.

Sutter failed, in other words, so that others might succeed.

When it comes to an interest in western American history, I was a distinctly late bloomer. Born and raised in Banning, California, between Riverside and Palm Springs, I was twenty-two years old and attending graduate school in Connecticut before western history caught my attention. Speaking of the services of historical image-makers and spin-doctors, I would like to have had a more clear and purposeful personal narrative to tell. I would like to be able to say that I became interested in western American history in earliest childhood. But there are too many witnesses to the contrary. My parents and my older sisters can testify that I did not bounce from the car on family vacations, eager to steep myself in the ambience of western historical sites. I suspect, though I cannot clearly remember, that we made a stop at Sutter's Fort, but I fear trustworthy memories would recall that I had to be pried from the car like a barnacle from a rock—a barnacle, in this case, protesting that she would really prefer to stay on the rock and read while the others saw the sites.

With this unfortunate personal history, I am in the market for someone to blame. I would like someone to hold responsible for the conviction that held me captive for my first twenty-two years, the conviction that western history was a very dull business. Searching for a possible villain, the eye falls on Sutter. Not, of course, the real Sutter—the man who abandoned his family in Switzerland, who traveled to Missouri, Santa Fé, Fort Vancouver, Alaska, Hawaii, and California, who exploited Indians in a manner uncompromised by mercy, who womanized and drank and bragged and lied in the grandest manner, who outdid Colorado's own Neil Bush in financial ineptness, and who lost his empire in a way that does indeed make him a prototype for failure.[1] Like any other normal human being, I find that Sutter quite interesting. I blame, instead, the fake Sutter, the dehumanized Sutter, the Sutter who had been washed, sanitized, bleached, shrunk to size, and thereby brought into compliance with the dullness standards of material suitable for schoolchildren, for tourists, and for residents of the city of Sacramento, where every imaginable hospital or health service seems to bear the patriarch's name—with "Sutter Psychiatric Services" having the most appealing historical resonance.

What happened to Sutter, of course, happened as well to western American history: a story of great drama and complexity became a dull and pious parable of a continent mastered and progress advanced, where a few failed so that others might succeed. Reversing that process of infused dullness at first seems impossible; it is a little like restoring circulation to a mummy. But this is where historical figures like Sutter are extremely helpful. Keeping him on a pedestal requires a constant struggle against the facts of his life. To let him off that pedestal and to restore him to full humanity, one simply has to cease to fight the facts and, instead, let the facts speak freely.

Over the last century, the facts of western history have had—and in some circles still have—a tough time of it. They barely start to speak for themselves when an anxious part of the audience immediately drowns them out with the cry, "How disillusioning! The facts will ruin our most treasured myths." But that is the happy part of life in the 1990s: it is increasingly clear, to the western public as well as to western historians, that we are not fighting a pointless war between western facts and western myths. We are, instead, engaged in a campaign to allow western facts to inspire western stories that can guide, instead of misguiding; stories that can lead, instead of misleading.

Let us review the facts of failure in Sutter's case. The common version of his story had him thriving and prospering, presiding over an inland empire of wheat and cattle, and then a flood of unprincipled gold-rushers swept in and stripped him of his property and his power. Sutter's failure, in this model, came completely from the outside. A plague of locusts swept down upon him, and what was worse, he had been kind and hospitable to these locusts, welcoming Anglo-Americans throughout the 1840s. And this is how they treated him—stealing his property and forcing him over the edge of failure.

And now the facts.[2] Long before the gold rush could push him there, Sutter had taken up permanent residence on the edge of failure. A family man with five children, he had reached a state of bankruptcy as a merchant in Switzerland. It only added a special note of poignancy to his troubles that his principal creditor appears to have been his unadmiring mother-in-law. He left Switzerland as a debtor, pursued by a warrant for his arrest. In America, he entered the Santa Fé trade and ended up on the losing side of that enterprise. Encouraging several Missouri acquaintances to invest in his venture, Sutter took a load of toys to New Mexico, and learned that New Mexicans did not particularly care for toys; nor did his Missouri acquaintances care for any more investment advice.

Arriving in Mexican California in 1839 and securing the governor's encouragement in the planting of an interior colony, Sutter seemed to be off to a genuinely fresh start, with his debts and creditors left far behind. Then, in 1841, he made the curious move of buying Fort Ross on the northern California coast from the Russians—buying, of course, only the buildings and livestock, because the Russians held no claim to the land. With this purchase, Sutter placed himself heavily in debt. Arrangements to pay off the debt in wheat, needed by the always hungry Russian-Alaskan colony at Sitka, only added new occasions for anxiety, as the precarious fortunes of wheat farming left Sutter with disappointing crops in several key years.

The Russians were not the only ones to take over the role once occupied by Sutter's mother-in-law: creditor with good prospects of getting a series of empty promises, and poor prospects of getting any actual repayment. A number of California merchants and ranchers advanced Sutter various goods—livestock, food, tools—and got in return a series of letters explaining why he could not pay them back yet. In these letters, Sutter sometimes played the role of innocent victim;

he was injured, he was maligned, by those who said he did not pay his debts. If there had been schools of business and management in the 1840s, and if Sutter had been recruited for the faculty, they would have made Sutter *swear* to keep his distance from the "financial management" courses, except, perhaps, on the one day a semester when he would be brought in as an example of how *not* to manage one's debts.

On the other side, Sutter's courses in "labor management" would have been sellouts. On this count, as Albert Hurtado shows elsewhere in this volume, Sutter was a clear success, recruiting, directing, coercing, and manipulating Indian labor. Sutter knew how to get Indians to herd cattle, construct buildings, tan hides, and plant and harvest wheat. But in this matter of demonstrated success, the floor has fallen out from under Sutter. Judged by one narrow set of standards as an economic success, this achievement, judged by another set of standards, appears as something of a moral failure. Even the business colleges of today, one has to hope, would be reluctant to use Sutter as a model of how to get the most out of a labor force.

And what about other spheres of achievement—say, the military? Sutter did succeed in the creation of an Indian militia, and when he chose to support the cause of Governor Micheltorena against the rebels in southern California, Sutter had the occasion to lead his Indian troops, as well as Euro-American troops, in a campaign. But the campaign was almost immediately a mess: Governor Micheltorena was an uncertain and slow commander; Sutter wasn't much better; the non-Indian troops soon began to desert; and Sutter's military career came to a halt when he surrendered to and briefly became the prisoner of the enemy.

Elbowed aside by John C. Frémont during the Bear Flag Rebellion, Sutter could not be a principal player in the conquest of California. Nonetheless, when he sponsored, indirectly and unintentionally, the discovery of gold in 1848, he seemed to be placed by providence at the center of opportunity, with chances to get in on the ground floor of both mining and merchandising. But Sutter did not seize the opportunity in merchandising, and his ventures into the gold country proved aimless and unproductive. He did, however, make some brief financial progress by turning his financial affairs over to his newly arrived Swiss son, a procedure of questionable legality that nonetheless led to the payment of many of his debts, including his longstanding

obligation to the Russians. But then relations with his son deterio-
rated, and Sutter resumed control of his estate. Trusting the estate to
the management of Peter Burnett led to a period when Sutter seemed
to be gaining ground financially, but then Sutter removed Burnett as
business agent. Submitting to the seductive proposals of speculators
and schemers, Sutter, step by step, did himself in.

It did not help, of course, that the United States government confirmed only one of Sutter's two land grants. The New Helvetia grant
stood, but the Sobrante grant, from the ill-fated Governor Micheltorena, was disallowed. Since Sutter had already sold parts of that second grant, he had to make good on those purchases with land from
the New Helvetia property, and this further reduced his holdings.

Were his successes, then, domestic and familial? Did the reunion
with his wife and surviving children, who joined him at long last in
California, permit Sutter at least a domestic variety of success? Abandoned in Switzerland for over fifteen years, his wife did not instantly
forgive and forget. Bearing the burden of managing his father's estate,
Sutter's eldest son mentally broke down under the strain, and finally
moved to Mexico to escape the burdens of life with his father. Sutter's
wife and daughter tried to contain his reckless hospitality, as well as his
drinking, and Sutter's second son Emil seemed to have his heart set on
being the maddest Sutter of all. When, in 1865, a disgruntled former
employee set the Sutters' Hock Farm home on fire and the Sutters decided to move to Washington, D.C., they did not leave a site hallowed
by happy family memories.

Why did they move to Washington? In 1865 John Sutter took up his
new, and final, career as a lobbyist. Unlike lobbyists who push for
wide causes and broad issues, Sutter had one interest to press on Congress: his own. From 1865 to 1880, virtually up to the moment of his
death, Sutter pleaded his case with Congress: he had welcomed Anglo-Americans to California; his help had, indeed, been crucial to the
U.S. takeover; and an ungrateful citizenry had taken his help, and left
him landless and powerless. A country that honored justice would
surely compensate him for his losses.

After several years in Washington, Sutter and his wife moved to a
small town in Pennsylvania, but he still traveled to Washington for
each session of Congress. With years of practice, Sutter and his cham-
pions produced a set piece, a formula, a litany, almost a kind of scrip-

ture of Sutter's life. Over a century and a half, many other westerners have approached life as if it were a great stage drama, in which they were assigned the part of the innocent victims. Miners, for instance, who intruded into Indian territory and then felt beleaguered and harassed by Indians defending their turf; or ambitious fortune-hunters who let their own exaggerated hopes lead them into improvident investments and who then denounced the cruel fate that had robbed them of their money: there are hundreds of variations on these western innocent victims, all of them chanting some variation on the theme "I only tried to make the most of an opportunity, and now look how I've been treated."[3]

Sutter had them all beat. Sutter was simply the best at constructing a version of his misfortunes in which everything was *done to him,* a version in which he bore no responsibility—beyond the admirable weakness of trusting and helping people.

It is the final capstone on the theme of failure that even this masterpiece of self-packaging did not work. While he did, for a time, secure a pension of $250 a month from the California State Legislature, Sutter never succeeded in his campaign for Congressional compensation. Just hours before he died in 1880, the most recent legislative session ended, and Sutter lost again.

It was this campaign for compensation, with the rhetorical demands it imposed, that drained the life out of Sutter's story. By the mid-1870s, Sutter and his friends had constructed a narrative which, if unsuccessful in moving Congress, was perfectly put together to bore western schoolchildren for a hundred years to come.

To see what had become of Sutter, to see how a colorful character had become monochrome, we can look at the proceedings of the Associated Pioneers of the Territorial Days of California, a group organized in February 1875 in New York City. The first thing that strikes the reader, in looking at the records of their annual meetings, is that writing speeches to deliver to this crowd was a pretty easy business. Every year, it seems, their speakers and toastmasters said what someone had said the year before. To write a toast or speech on the subject of John Sutter, you simply chose from a standard list of phrases and assembled them in the order you preferred.

These were the parts in the speech assembly-kit from which the Associated Pioneers chose their words:

great fame and services to California and to the Republic
good and noble old Pioneer
pioneer and philanthropist
mentor and protector of Indians
hospitable welcome
courtly gentleman and benefactor
the benefits which he conferred upon California, our country,
     and all mankind
inestimable services for his fellow man
the great Patriarch of our tribe
the revered chieftain of our clan
genial hospitality and unselfish generosity
pure character and spotless integrity
kindness and charity
liberal and generous to a fault
noble deeds and golden virtues
honorable and unselfish devotion to humanity
noblest of men
noble Patriarch
the beauty, purity and bravery of his life
the nobility of his nature
the purity and nobleness of his character[4]

The pattern of language and reference here is not a subtle one. When the publication of the Associated Pioneers records the fact, for instance, that "Jos. S. Spinney, Esq. . . . delivered a fervid and beautiful tribute to [Sutter,] the great and good Pioneer, but there is no record of the same, and [it] cannot, after this lapse of time, be reproduced,"[5] one does not feel an overpowering sense of loss. Unless there was more to Jos. S. Spinney, Esq., than we presently realize, it is a pretty sure thing that the words *noble* and *patriarch* figured prominently in Spinney's "fervid and beautiful tribute."

Sutter himself attended some of these meetings. It strikes me as something of a wonder that in the midst of all these tributes to his integrity, Christian charity, and, of all things, purity, he did not finally exclaim: "This is all extremely kind, but I think you've got the wrong fellow." But we are, with these tributes, clearly in the presence of ritual belief, belief that Sutter had evidently come to share himself. In this formulaic story, every other element of Sutter's history disappeared, and only two facts remained: he had welcomed and aided arriving emigrants; and he had sponsored an undertaking, the construction of a mill, which surprised everyone by turning up gold. Those two facts gave him indisputable standing as a great agent of the Manifest Destiny of the United States, and thereby made all other facts dismissible.

Following Sutter's death, the San José *Pioneer* derived from those two facts a wonderfully improbable summation of Sutter's career and character: "Truly he was in all respects a Christian, and his every act through life was that of true Christianity. . . ."[6]

This business of western mythmaking is indeed a wonderful thing. Religion, Christian or any other, does not seem to have figured much in Sutter's life in California, but so what? A man almost constitutionally unable to keep his obligations and pay his debts, a man whose use and abuse of women remains unsettling and disheartening—such a man nonetheless can be spruced up and launched on the road to sainthood, sent out to personify nobility, integrity, purity, and even Christianity. Perhaps the height of improbability comes with the comparison of Sutter to Jesus Christ. Speaking to the Associated Pioneers in New York, Sutter's friend General H. G. Gibson drew a remarkable picture of Sutter facing death "with no bitterness or anger in his heart, only a sorrowful reproach in the spirit of the prayer of the Divine Master: 'Father! forgive them for they know not what they do.'"[7] Sutter on his deathbed; Christ on his cross—and yet, by some miracle, General Gibson finished his speech and was not struck down by lightning in midsentence.

In a book that is as fascinating as it is maddening, *The Fatal Environment: The Myth of the Frontier in the Age of Industrialization, 1800–1890,* the literary scholar Richard Slotkin applies similar thinking to the death of George Armstrong Custer. Custer's death, Slotkin argues, fits the fundamental patterns of Christian thought. Custer's death was, to white Americans in the 1870s, a sacrifice that redeemed and revitalized his nation; Custer's death thus mirrored Christ's.[8] When I first read Slotkin's book, I found this analogy unpersuasive. But now, after a tour of duty with the Associated Pioneers of California, listening to them celebrate Sutter's virtues and lament his many injuries, Slotkin's analysis is harder to deny. If nostalgic Americans could cast Sutter as a trusting lamb sacrificed so that others might prosper, then it would be no particular struggle to provide the same intellectual service to Custer, a man who was surely Sutter's equal in saintliness.

"Father! forgive them for they know not what they do" was not a sentiment Sutter expressed in real life. On the contrary, in Sutter's long campaign in Washington, D.C., years in which he became one of the most familiar characters around the Capitol, forgiveness did not figure in what he asked of Congress. Keeping the memory of his injuries alive was his principal cause. This was a man who had learned to treasure his wounds, virtually to savor the contrast between what he was in the past and what he had been reduced to in the present. It is, indeed, important to note that others have been considerably more reduced. As Richard Dillon wrote of Sutter's last years, his "circumstances were comfortable, although he had to pose as a destitute petitioner in his memorials to Congress." He and his wife built a "fine brick home" in Pennsylvania.[9] But fine brick home or not, the contrast between what he had had in the 1840s (or what he would have had in the 1840s if he had ever gotten his empire clear of debts) and his reduced state in the 1870s was so galling that he could not adopt the Christ-like resignation that his eulogist later attributed to him.

Much more accurate in capturing Sutter's feelings was the statement he made to the historian H. H. Bancroft, a ringing summation of the Innocent Victim's view of the world:

> I have been robbed and ruined by lawyers and politicians. My men were crushed by the iron heel of civilization; my cattle were driven off by hungry gold-seekers; my fort and mills were deserted and left to decay; my lands were squatted on by overland immigrants; and, finally, I was cheated out of all my property. All Sacramento was once mine.[10]

You will notice here that wonder of human expression, the passive-voice verb—by which everything *was done* to Sutter, and Sutter did *nothing* to himself. His failure came upon him like a blow from the sky; his own failures in financial management were gone, erased, stricken from the record by the wretched behavior of the gold-rushers.

There is nothing particularly surprising in Sutter's choice of historical explanations. One could logically ask Congress for compensation if one's misfortunes stemmed from the cruel and ungrateful acts of others. It would be a lot tougher to ask for compensation on the basis of injury done to oneself *by* oneself, by one's own acts of improvident and misguided management. (In our time, of course, this formulation changes; one can barely begin to imagine the rich possibilities that the savings and loan bailout would have presented to Sutter and his political strategists.)

No wonder Sutter adopted an innocent victim's formulation of his own history. What might seem considerably more surprising is that his society confirmed and supported him in that creative and selective reading of his experience. But this is only briefly surprising: Sutter's story fit smoothly inside that great, vanity-satisfying myth of American destiny. By pioneering settlement in the California interior, welcoming and aiding American arrivals, he had been on the side of the angels (or, at the least, of the Anglos). He could, therefore, be indulged and supported in his assertion that he was the victim of outsiders, when he should have been the beneficiary of their gratitude.

In a terrible act of unconscious ingratitude on my part, my work *The Legacy of Conquest* made absolutely no mention—in text, footnotes, or bibliography—of the name Josiah Royce. Born during the gold rush, Josiah Royce grew up in California and went on to become a philosopher at Harvard. At his request, his mother, Sarah Royce, wrote down her memories of the overland trail and of gold-rush California, and this text reveals her to have been an uncompromisingly moral person. Sarah Royce, a woman who lived every day of her life with religious thoughts in her mind, would have been nonplussed by the notion of John Sutter as an exemplary Christian.

Very much his mother's child, Josiah Royce in 1886 published a study of his home state's history, *California: From the Conquest in 1846 to the Second Vigilance Committee in San Francisco: A Study of American Character*.[11] Note the timing: 1886, seven years before Frederick Jackson Turner would draw on his memories of childhood in Wisconsin to offer his version of western, or more accurately, midwestern, history, "The Significance of the Frontier in American History." Josiah Royce put forward his model of western expansion seven years before Turner did. And yet, for reasons that stem mostly from national pride, Turner caught on and became the father of western history, and Royce, though renowned as a philosopher, held no standing in western history.[12]

Royce always used the word *conquest* freely and honestly; while something short of a model in his awareness of Indian history, he was fully aware that Hispanic people were established in the Far West long before Anglos arrived. Royce's facing up to the fact of conquest very much influenced me in my younger days; by my older days, I had pushed that influence to the edge of awareness, and I completely failed to include an acknowledgment of my debt to him in *Legacy*. You only hurt the ones you love, I suppose; in any case, I take this opportunity to make up for that sin of omission in *Legacy*.

Josiah Royce is Exhibit # 1 in the proposition that what we now call the New Western History has its own distinguished history.[13] Look through his California book, and it is clear that a critical appraisal of western expansion did not begin in the 1960s. But it is indeed the affirmation that the historian should think hard and critically that sets apart the New Western Historians, as well as Josiah Royce, from the traditional, not particularly reflective, western historians who dominated the field through most of this century.

When Royce wrote his California book, the cult of Sutter was fully developed. If he had wanted to, Royce could have joined the chorus of celebration, acclaiming Sutter as the vital instrument in the civilizing of California. Instead, and very characteristically for Royce, he thought hard about Sutter and then wrote a few brief, but essential sentences:

> In character Sutter was an affable and hospitable visionary, of hazy ideas, with a great liking for popularity, and with a mania for undertaking too much. A heroic figure he was not, although his romantic position as pioneer in the great valley made him seem so to many travelers and historians. When the gold-seekers later came, the ambitious Sutter utterly lost his head and threw away all his truly wonderful opportunities. He, however, also suffered many things from the injustice of the newcomers. He died a few years since in poverty, complaining bitterly of American ingratitude. He should undoubtedly have been better treated by most of our countrymen, but if he was often wronged, he was also often in the wrong, and his fate was the ordinary one of the persistent and unteachable dreamer. He remained to the end a figure more picturesque than manly in our California life.[14]

We did not have to wait for Josiah Royce to come along to find nineteenth-century observers who saw the weaknesses in Sutter's claims on paradise. In 1846 the Swiss immigrant Heinrich Lienhard traveled overland to California. Like many other overland travelers,

Lienhard saw his arrival at Sutter's Fort as a landmark in his life. But the passage in which he described his arrival captures the complexity of western history, captures the obligation, still before us, to push beyond celebration to the writing of a clear, honest record.

"It was," Lienhard wrote,

> one of the happiest moments of my life, as I stood there and gazed at my actual, my final destination. After passing several more adobe corrals, [we] reached the main gate of the fort. There a gruesome sight met my eyes: the long, black hair and skull of an Indian dangling from one of the gateposts.[15]

This display of a defeated enemy was a long-running tradition in the battles that punctuated the invasion and conquest of North America. In this case, the sight echoed an even more long-running tradition in the thought and literature of European civilization—the death's head in the garden, included in many of the classic paintings of Western civilization. "*Et in arcadia ego*" is the announcement Death makes in this tradition; "I, too, am in paradise."

Signing up to work for Sutter, Heinrich Lienhard cultivated a garden. In 1848, when James Marshall had made his gold discovery, Lienhard felt pulled to the mines. But he had devoted himself to his garden, and "finally I abandoned the idea of going to the mines; I did not believe I could be happy away from my plants."[16] So Lienhard stayed and worked in his garden, a type of labor that gave him great pleasure. But then came a return of the "*Et in arcadia ego*" theme, Death's reliable announcement, "I, too, am in paradise."

"By May twentieth," Lienhard wrote,

> my potatoes were in bloom, and my grain was three or four feet high. That morning when I woke up the air seemed unusually chilly. When I got out of bed to my surprise I found the grass covered with frost. My hopes vanished into thin air. . . .
>
> After the sun was up, I inspected my plants and found that every melon, tomato, bean, and cucumber I had set was dead and black. Potatoes that were in full bloom yesterday were now frozen to within six inches of the ground; tall green grain that was about to ripen had turned into a few shriveled ends. . . . My vines, that had been thick with grapes the size of small bullets, were dropping.[17]

Not a man of excessive sanguinity on any occasion, Lienhard was one of many nineteenth-century westerners who did not deny the facts of failure. He would not fudge his description of the risk of frost in the theoretically Arcadian environment of California; he would not puff himself up for a windy proclamation announcing that this year's melons, potatoes, and grapes had frozen so that next year's crops might prosper.

In the same spirit, Lienhard would not join in the canonization of Sutter. When he first met Sutter, Lienhard was enchanted: "as I listened to his pithy conversation, to his tales so highly colored with romance and adventure, I was spell bound." Sutter was, Lienhard wrote, "an incredibly entertaining talker, and for the time being at least, I believed it all, in spite of myself." Over time, Lienhard learned that a number of Sutter's tales—stories, for instance, of his service in the Swiss-French army—were colorful fibs. Sutter's drinking problems, Sutter's callous treatment of Indians, Sutter's use of Indian women and girls, Sutter's unpaid debts, Sutter's susceptibility to flatterers and swindlers, Sutter's conflicts with his family: Lienhard's portrait included all the details that grounded Sutter as a three-dimensional human being, not an ethereal and dull pioneer saint.[18]

Summing up the pious and sanitized version of Sutter's character, his friend Colonel I. S. Tichenor wrote: of Sutter "it may truly be said: 'A more noble man never lived.'"[19] Lienhard's down-to-earth stories convey an immeasurably greater vitality and interest. Consider the human reality in this encounter with Sutter's vanity: "I owned a pair of black trousers [Sutter] wanted to buy," Lienhard reported, "and I knew I would not have any peace until I complied with his request." Lienhard finally set a high price, and to his surprise, Sutter paid it. "But his hips were larger than mine, and the first day he wore the trousers they split when he sat down and leaned over suddenly."[20]

In his old age, Sutter had erased these embarrassments and failures from his record, and perhaps from his memory. He constructed, instead, a simplified and sanctified version of his character. He created a story of his past in which he was riding on a one-way, nonstop, direct trajectory to success until the gold rush threw him off track. "When I settled first in the Sacramento Valley," he wrote in 1879 to a supporter, "then I thought to make me a home for life, and I would have become one of the wealthiest Citizens on the Pacific, but the discovery of the gold, has destroyed all my enterprises and plans and bad designing men, swindlers and thieves, and even the courts treated me very badly & unjust."[21]

If it had not been for the gold rush, Sutter said several times, he would have been the richest man in California. Nostalgic imagining aside, before gold ever appeared in the mill race at Coloma, Sutter had encountered frustration, disappointment, and failure. He had a world of evidence to tell him that the pursuit of fortune in newly conquered areas is a very uncertain matter, that short-term successes, in these circumstances, have a way of evolving into long-term failures. The conquest of natives and nature was, and is, a risk-filled and precarious operation. Trying to ride westward expansion, Sutter's experience showed, was often enough the prelude to getting bucked by westward expansion. Serving as the host for American colonization, Sutter evidently thought he had this force under control.

Later, lost in the contemplation of his own injuries, Sutter could not take seriously the story of his failure, with all its historical lessons. At long last, thanks to the changing currents of western American life, we are ready to learn the lessons that Sutter chose to forget. Said so memorably at Sutter's Fort a year or two ago, the proposition "Men! They never change" is now open for rethinking.

Notes

1. On the chance that fame is indeed fleeting, it may be worth noting that Neil Bush was the son of President George Bush, and that he served on the board of directors of Silverado Savings and Loan, one of the more disastrous savings and loan institutions. In 1991, Neil Bush moved from Denver.

2. Sutter's biography is available in Richard Dillon, *Fool's Gold: The Decline and Fall of Captain John Sutter of California* (New York: Coward-McCann, 1967; reprint, Santa Cruz, California: Western Tanager, 1981).

3. Chapter 1 in Limerick, *The Legacy of Conquest: The Unbroken Past of the American West* (New York: W. W. Norton, 1987) takes up this theme. Regrettably I did not think to include Sutter, despite his perfect fit.

4. Associated Pioneers of the Territorial Days of California, *A Nation's Benefactor: Gen'l John A. Sutter: Memorial of His Life and Public Services, and an Appeal to Congress, to Citizens of California, and the People of the United States, by his Fellow Pioneers of California* (New York: Polydore Barnes, Printer, 1880).

5. Associated Pioneers of Territorial Days, *A Nation's Benefactor,* p. 12.

6. Reprinted in Associated Pioneers of Territorial Days, *A Nation's Benefactor,* p. 24.

7. Associated Pioneers of Territorial Days, *A Nation's Benefactor,* p. 13.

8. Richard Slotkin, *The Fatal Environment: The Myth of the Frontier in the Age of Industrialization, 1800–1890* (New York: Atheneum, 1985).

9. Dillon, *Fool's Gold,* p. 346.

10. Sutter, quoted by Hubert Howe Bancroft in Dillon, *Fool's Gold,* p. 347.

11. Josiah Royce, *California: From the Conquest in 1846 to the Second Vigilance Committee in San Francisco: A Study of American Character* (Boston: Houghton, Mifflin and Company, 1886; reprint, Santa Barbara: Peregrine Publishers, Inc., 1970).

12. In *Josiah Royce* (Norman: University of Oklahoma Press, 1991), Robert Hine at long last gives Royce his proper consideration as a western intellectual.

13. For an exploration of the New Western History, see Patricia Nelson Limerick, Clyde A. Milner II, and Charles E. Rankin, eds., *Trails: Toward a New Western History* (Lawrence: University Press of Kansas, 1991).

14. Royce, *California,* p. 34.

15. Heinrich Lienhard, *A Pioneer at Sutter's Fort, 1846–1850: The Adventures of Heinrich Lienhard,* trans. and ed. Marguerite Eyer Wilbur (Los Angeles: Calafia Society, 1941), p. 3.

16. Lienhard, *A Pioneer at Sutter's Fort,* p. 122.

17. Lienhard, *A Pioneer at Sutter's Fort,* p. 123.

18. Lienhard, *A Pioneer at Sutter's Fort,* pp. 5, 9, 67, 74–75, 154–55, 68, 75–76, 84, 93–94, 110, 159, 148–52, and 198.

19. Colonel Tichenor to Annie Bidwell, July 13, 1880, in *John A. Sutter's Last Days: The Bidwell Letters,* ed. Allan R. Ottley (Sacramento: Sacramento Book Collectors Club, 1986), p. 47.

20. Lienhard, *A Pioneer at Sutter's Fort,* p. 79.

21. Sutter to Smith Rudd, December 26, 1879, Rudd Manuscripts, Lilly Library, Indiana University, Bloomington, Indiana.

The Contributors

Iris H. W. Engstrand, professor of history and director of Hispanic studies at the University of San Diego, is the author of many scholarly works related to California and the Spanish Borderlands. She currently has in progress a comprehensive account of the Spanish and Mexican era in California history. Her study of John Sutter's career has included research on the neglected early portion of his life in Switzerland.

Albert L. Hurtado is associate professor and director of graduate studies in history at Arizona State University. The author of *Indian Survival on the California Frontier* (1985), he traces his interest in John Sutter and Sutter's Indian relations to class tours of Sutter's Fort during his grade-school years in Sacramento.

Howard R. Lamar is Sterling Professor of History emeritus at Yale University. Demonstrating a long concern with the role of frontier entrepreneurs such as John Sutter, his publications include *The Trader on the American Frontier: Myth's Victim* (1977). Professor Lamar has recently served as president of Yale University.

Patricia Nelson Limerick, professor of history at the University of Colorado, Boulder, is the author of *Desert Passages: Encounters with the American Desert* (1985) and *The Legacy of Conquest: The Unbroken Past of the American West* (1987). She is also the senior editor of *Trails: Toward a New Western History* (1991), a collection of interpretive essays that indicate the major reappraisal now under way in historical thought about the American West.

Kenneth N. Owens, organizer of the Sutter lectures and editor of this volume, is professor of history and director of the Capital Campus Public History program at California State University, Sacramento. He first became interested in John Sutter in 1977 while conducting research for the creation of a new regional history museum in Sacramento.

Richard White, professor of history at the University of Washington, is an outstanding exponent of western environmental history. His recent publications include *The Middle Ground: Indians, Empires and Republics in the Great Lakes Region, 1650–1815* (1991) and *'It's Your Misfortune and None of My Own': A New History of the American West* (1991).

Index